FIRMLY PLANTED PUBLICATIONS
An imprint of Equipped for Life Ministries, Dallas, Texas

I0112118

Freedom through the Cross

The cross in God's Plan

B. Dale Taliaferro

Freedom through the Cross
published by Firmly Planted Publications
an imprint of Equipped for Life Ministries

Copyright © 2015 by B. Dale Taliaferro
International Standard Book Number:
978-1-950072-11-8

Cover Art by Hannah Gleghorn Design, Frisco, Texas

Printed copies sold at Logos Book Store, 6620 Snider Plaza,
Dallas, Texas, 75205-3483

For information:
Equipped for Life Ministries
P.O. Box 12013
Dallas, Texas 75225
U.S.A.

Library of Congress Number:

First Edition / First Printing / 2015

Table of Contents

Preface to the Revised Edition

This series of books was written during my spiritual journey. As a result, I now find the need to go back through each volume and make some necessary corrections and updates. I really didn't understand how many preconceived ideas that I was working from and that were still hindering my comprehension of the real message of the Bible. I still needed to confront several issues and hold them under the microscope of God's Word. For the sake of simplicity, I will summarize those issues here:

1. I developed a better understanding of the historical situations of some very important passages which changed my thinking relative to their meaning. As a result, the unpardonable sin has been revised. Basically, the unpardonable sin is a rejection of Jesus as the Messiah by the first century Jewish people, resulting in a delay of their earthly kingdom, promised to them by God in the OT, and to their missing entering into that kingdom in their mortal bodies.

2. I finally was able to move past my theological prejudices concerning Acts 16:31 and Eph. 2:8-9 by understanding salvation and faith Biblically. As a result, I have found that the Bible does not describe a person as being saved from hell because salvation never refers to a deliverance from hell once-for-all or in any other way. Consequently, these two classic passages on salvation have nothing to do with a rescue from hell with a promise of heaven. Those ideas have been read into these passages without any substantiation.

3. Since no one was ever described as a "saved person" by *initially* trusting in Jesus, I am led to reframe from doing that as well. I eventually realized that even the apostles were not described as "saved persons" after they

1

had initially trusted in Jesus. *Salvation is not a standing or status before God that guarantees a person a heavenly home and an escape from hell.* Nor is it a permanent, unchangeable condition that is reached by initially (or continually) trusting in Jesus. We can be saved from temptations and sins, but we can't be saved from hell and given heaven due to a simple trust in Jesus.

4. Finally, I realized that while there is no concept in the NT that can be likened to the traditional idea of a "saved person" in Christian teachings, there is a NT concept of a *salvation that is taking place presently.* As a result, it is biblical to describe people as being saved from temptations and sins but not as having been saved once for all from hell with a guarantee of heaven. Since the Bible doesn't do that, neither should we. It is easy to see how this reinforces the new understanding of Acts 16:30-31 and Eph. 2:8-9.

With these discoveries, I was able to reach a consistent concept of salvation with nothing but the Bible as my guide. **The biggest correction that I have needed in these volumes is to distinguish between a *spiritual* salvation that is defined as an ongoing deliverance from temptations and sins from the traditional, but mistaken, idea of a *spiritual* salvation that supposedly takes place at the moment of initial faith in Jesus and that supposedly obtains a deliverance from hell.** While the former is clearly Biblical; the latter is a creation by men alone.

2

Preface

We have heard that Jesus died for our sins. And He did.[1]

We have heard that Jesus paid a satisfaction to the Father. And He did.[2]

We have heard that Jesus' payment is completely sufficient in itself to pay for all of man's sins. And it is.[3]

We have heard that involved in that payment was the reconciliation of the whole world. And it was.[4]

We have heard that believing in Jesus obtains the forgiveness of sins. And … well … I don't know. Does it?[5]

This book will explain that the death of Christ did more than pay a satisfaction to the Father and a ransom for sin (to whom … the Bible never says). There was much more grace involved in the death of Jesus than the grace needed for forgiveness. Some of this boundless grace of God is what I hope to bring before the reader for his consideration. The ramifications of God's grace provided in His Son's death are world shattering. They will force us to think beyond the confines of our current theological orthodoxy and view the whole world in a different light altogether.

---

[1] 1Cor. 15:1-5.

[2] 1John 2:2; 4:10.

[3] John 19:30. But after reviewing this passage independently, I have concluded that it was not suggesting that Jesus' payment was "a full one," but rather "one that fulfilled" the OT demands and more.

[4] 2Cor. 5:18-20.

[5] John 8:24 and Acts 10:42-43 do not establish what orthodox Christian theology requires in the area of forgiveness. These forgivenesses both have to do with one sin alone, namely that of rejecting Jesus as Messiah. Neither passage deals with all of man's sins, much less with any of his future sins which must have a forgiveness even before they occur in order for Christian theology to be sufficient.

In the two volumes that follow, help will be given to work out some of those ramifications together. The volume entitled *A Shrinking World Requires a Better Christianity* will focus of some of the necessary changes that we must make in order to keep our faith relevant as we deal cross-culturally as we have never done before. I hope you will be as excited at the prospects of this study as I am. May the Lord bless these books in aiding you in reaching the world for Christ to the glory of the Father.

Chapter 1

What We Can All Agree On

There is an old saying that warns people not to *throw out the baby with the bath water*. That idiom graphically warns the hearer not to reject the good, the essential, or the true elements when he is trying to get rid of the bad, the inessential, or the false elements in a given situation. There are so many Biblical facts that must not be thrown out even though there are some *assumptions*, posing as Biblical facts, that must be rejected. Here are the "baby facts" that we all ought to agree upon:

1. Jesus died to deal with man's sins (among other things).[1]
2. Jesus's death satisfied the Father (propitiated Him).[2]
3. Jesus's death bought (redeemed) man.[3]
4. Jesus's death makes reconciliation (with God) possible.[4]
5. Jesus' death is completely sufficient.[5]

These facts must never be relinquished. They represent the clear statements of the Bible. The problem, however, is that these facts are surrounded by *assumptions*, logical extrapolations from the facts, that can't be supported from the text of Scripture. The reader and student of the Bible along with the listener of sermons and Sunday school lessons must develop a discerning spirit to keep from accepting the unsupportable premises often taught with the soteriological (salvific) themes of Scripture and

---

[1] John 1:29; 1Cor. 15:3; Eph. 1:7.
[2] Heb. 10:5-14; 1John 2:2; 4:10.
[3] Mk. 10:45; 1Cor. 6:19-20; Gal. 3:13.
[4] 2Cor. 5:18-20; Col. 1:21-23.
[5] Rom. 6:8-10; Heb. 10:12-14, 18.

cling only to the Biblical facts.

Let's look at the five Biblical postulates listed above to demonstrate the point being made. The important thing to understand is God holds each of us responsible for critiquing what we read and hear. If we receive unbiblical ideas as Biblical facts, those unbiblical ideas will surely influence how we understand the people with whom we come in contact and how we respond to the circumstances that confront us. When we are guided by unsound ideas, however much sense and wisdom they may appear to have, we are sure to respond unsoundly. These responses have the power to blaspheme the name (character) of God rather than praise Him.

Some of the reasons that the Spirit of God was given to believers in Jesus Christ are 1.) to create love for the heart to express,[1] 2.) to instill power to enable the will,[2] and 3.) to grant a sound mind.[3] From a sound mind flow sound practices. When we remember that we will be judged in the afterlife according to the responses that we give as we live life now and not according to some unified code of beliefs that all men are expected to possess, we realize how important the connection is between right thinking and right actions. As a result, the apostle Paul told the Christians at Rome to allow the Spirit of God to transform them as they renewed their minds with the truth of God. Right thinking produces right attitudes, and these two things together produce right character as Dr. Earl Radmacher used to tell us.

The first Biblical tenet listed above is that Jesus died *to deal with man's sins*. That is supported by several passages, exemplified in 1Cor. 15:3:

---

[1] Rom. 5:5; Gal. 5:22.
[2] Eph. 4:13; Gal. 5:16-17.
[3] 2Tim. 1:7.

"For I delivered to you as of first importance what I also received, that Christ died *for our sins* according to the Scriptures ..."

Jesus, who was the Christ of God,[1] died for sins. This fact is undeniable if one believes that the Bible is God's Word to man. "Christ died for our sins." He came as the Lamb of God to take away the sins that have separated man from God in this life.

But it is not really the fact that Christ died for man's sins that is debated by evangelicals. The question that is debated is, "*For what purpose* or *to what end* did Jesus die for the sins of man?"

Did He die to save a person from hell? Was that His purpose in dying?

Did He die to pay (and thus forgive) the penalty of eternal condemnation that is *supposed* to be resting upon man because of his sins? Was that the goal that He accomplished in His death?

Did He die so that He could offer a place in heaven to the one who believes in Him?

Did He die so that the "believer" might have not only a place in heaven but assurance of that possession?

We are not debating the Biblical fact that Jesus died "for sins." We all believe that. We are debating the purpose or the end goal that He wanted to reach when He died to deal with man's sins. Does His purpose or end goal secure a blessed afterlife or an enriched present life? Or both? The answer that a person gives here is crucially important for himself and for each person with whom he shares Jesus.

The second Biblical proposition listed above is Jesus' death satisfied or propitiated the Father. This supposition seems to be clearly stated in 1John 4:10:

"In this is love, not that we loved God, but that He loved us and

---

[1] John 1:38, 41; Acts 9:19-22.

sent *His Son [to be the] propitiation for our sins*." (my emphasis)

God the Father sent His Son to propitiate Himself. That this propitiation has to do with the sins man commits is clearly stated by John both here and earlier in this same letter:

> "... and *He Himself is the propitiation for our sins*; and not for ours only, but also for those of the whole world." (1Jn. 2:2, my emphasis)

But care needs to be taken here since in neither passage does it say that it is the death of Christ that propitiates the Father. Rather it is Christ Jesus Himself. He is the propitiation for sins. Of course, some may argue that since the life is in the blood, the propitiation of the Father is accomplished when Jesus gave Himself up to death.[1] But it should not be forgotten that it is all important *who* died for man's sins to propitiate the Father.

Now whether the propitiation is found in Jesus's life or in Jesus' death, it doesn't change anything that is being suggested in the argument of this book. It may lend itself, however, to a better and more emphatic emphasis upon living the Christian life if *the propitiation is in the life that Jesus gives for living pleasingly before the Father.* And that is the goal of both the life of Christ and His death. It is also the focal point that should permeate our messages: *in whatever way the death of Jesus propitiates the Father, it is for the end that men may live lives pleasing to Him.* Propitiation has nothing to do with the afterlife as far as we know from these texts of Scripture (nor any other Biblical mention of propitiation). Propitiation satisfies God so that He is reconciled to man and able to forgive man's sins when he desires to return to Him. But since there is a recompense for all evil and worthless deeds,[2] it is obvious that the propitiation that Jesus provided in His

---

[1] John 10:17-18; Gen. 9:4-7.
[2] Eccl. 12:13-14; 2Cor. 5:10.

death has no affect in the day of judgment.

So, no one is debating that Jesus satisfied or propitiated the Father concerning the sins of mankind. But once again, to what end or for what purpose did He propitiate the Father?

Did He propitiate the Father so that the one who believes in Jesus can live with Him forever in heaven?

Did He propitiate the Father so that He, being the Judge of the whole world, might remove His anger from the believer and forgive the eternal penalty that *supposedly* rests upon him for his sins?

In short, what does the propitiation of Jesus actually accomplish? Therein lies the ground for debate.

The third Biblical truth listed above affirms that Jesus paid a ransom to liberate man when He gave up His life in death. All agree with these facts because they are transparently stated in the Scriptures. So, for example, 1Pet. 1:18-19 tell us what God's plan for Jesus was when He went to the cross. Peter wrote,

> "… you were redeemed … with precious blood, as of a lamb unblemished and spotless, the blood of Christ." (emphasis mine)

Everyone basically agrees with this direct statement of Scripture. That is not the place where the debate rises up to divide the people of God. The debate is over the *assumptions* that have been included in the doctrine of redemption but that are not found specifically in God's Word. While our logic often takes us beyond the explicit statements of God's Word, it is only God's explicit statements that keep us safe. So, let's ask:

From what is a person redeemed?

Is he redeemed from hell?

Is he redeemed from Satan?

From sin?

From all of these objects?

To whom was the redemptive price paid?

Is redemption a once-for-all phenomenon?

The problem is that the relative silence by God's Word does not keep us from our dogmatism.

The fourth Biblical fact states that Jesus' death makes reconciliation with God possible. Every evangelical that I know believes that truth. Rom. 5:10 says,

> "For if, while we were enemies, we *were reconciled to God* through the death of His Son, much more *having been reconciled,* we shall be saved by His life." (emphases mine)

It should be noted here that while the reconciliation is described as a past event, the salvation that is mentioned is future. Furthermore, reconciliation has to do with the death of Jesus while the salvation in Paul's mind has to do with the life of Jesus. Plainly, these two issues, reconciliation and salvation, are not the same thing in the book of Romans.

The salvation to which Paul is referring in Romans no one in two thousand years has experienced. It is the physical deliverance accomplished at the return of the Jewish Messiah to earth. And that deliverance is conditioned upon God's people living righteously before the Lord returns. No one has been saved in this way for the simple reason that Jesus has not returned. But He is coming back, and each person will give an account concerning how he lived his life at that time. A good report will admit him into Messiah's kingdom on earth.

Like the other truths, this one has *assumptions* flowing from it that find little support in the Scriptures.

So, for example, is reconciliation a once-for-all phenomenon?

When does reconciliation occur?

What are the conditions that must be met for reconciliation to occur?

When someone is reconciled to God what exactly does that mean to the person?

How does that affect his life?

Is reconciliation a status or standing, or is it a relationship that has been reestablished with God?

Does reconciliation assume a previous relationship that had been broken off and is now in need of mending?

Or does reconciliation denote a new relationship altogether?

The fifth truth, that Jesus' death is completely sufficient, is received by all evangelicals. Yet many display confusion in their attempt to understand how some of the commands of Scripture relate to it. So, for example, one group believes that Christ's death is sufficient to pay for their sins and get them to heaven, but they still need to persevere in their faith. If they don't persevere in their faith, they will, after all is said and done, miss heaven altogether. If Christ's death is sufficient, one wonders why perseverance is still needed.

We've heard and read the answers given to that question for the last five hundred years, but nothing seems to dispel the uneasiness of having to balance an all-sufficient payment by Christ with the need for continuing in the faith. If Christ did it all *at the cross*, if His payment was all-sufficient (meeting every requirement) to get a person to heaven, why is there a need to do something more (like persevering in the faith) after believing in Christ's all-sufficient work? Wouldn't it really be nice to find just one clear verse that says unless a person believes in Jesus and perseveres in his faith to the end of his life he cannot go to heaven? There is not one verse that says that. Every verse, that is

11

understood to propagate those truths, has to be read through a grid of multiple *assumptions*. We will be better followers of Christ when we come to the point where we recognize facts from assumptions.

Another group believes that Christ's death is sufficient to pay for their sins and get them to heaven, but they still need to be obedient. This group on the surface at least seems to believe the same thing as the last group. But there is a difference. These believe that if they don't persevere they will lose what they had gained by believing in Christ. The other group believes that if a person doesn't persevere in his faith, he never truly believed at all. In that case, the non-persevering person doesn't lose what he had gained by believing in Christ. He never truly believed in Christ so he never gained anything in the first place. *If Christ's death is really sufficient, one wonders why it wouldn't cover the lapse in obedience that might follow believing in Christ's all-sufficient payment on the cross.*

The point in this whole discussion is this: while most Christians adhere to the five truths that we began with, many have *assumed* other propositions to be true that are related to these initial five truths. But these *assumptions*, although they may be eminently logical and thoroughly reasonable, are, nonetheless, questionable because they find no support in the *explicit* statements of the Bible. Their only basis is the reason of the men who have formulated them, deducing concepts that fit their preconceived, theological grid for understanding the Bible.

Let's not forget that when we stand before the Judgment Seat of Christ, He will ask us about our stewardship of God's Word.[1] At that time we will give an account for how we learned

---

[1] 1Cor. 4:1-2; 11:1.

it, how we lived it,[1] and how we passed it on to others.[2] I wonder what the *recompense* for that failed stewardship will be? James warned the churches in the letter he wrote to the dispersed followers of Jesus, saying,

> "Let not many of you become teachers, my brethren, knowing that as such we shall incur *a stricter judgment.*" (Js. 3:1)

Teachers can and do lead others astray, *intentionally* and *unwittingly*. The first is deplorable; the second understandable. But both are equally culpable. It takes hard work to get to the truth of the Scriptures, but, on the other hand, it is so easy to pass on what other, respected teachers have said without questioning their premises or their conclusions. We are commanded to do the former;[3] we are foolish to do the latter.[4]

But lest what has just been said frighten anyone into *not* teaching, he should balance what has been said with these familiar verses:

> "Go therefore and *make disciples* of all the nations, baptizing them in the name of the Father and the Son and the Holy Spirit, *teaching them* to observe all that I commanded you; and lo, I am with you always, even to the end of the age." (Matt. 28:19-20, emphases mine)

What has been called the Great Commission by the editors of our English Bibles is Jesus' instruction, expressing His will that His closest disciples would *make disciples* from every nation under the sun. We need to be clear on an assumption that has pervaded the interpretation of the Great Commission for a very long time. That assumption is that Jesus commanded His disci-

---

[1] Matt. 4:4; John 17:17; Ps. 119.
[2] Matt. 28:19; 2Tim. 1:13-14; 2:1-2.
[3] 2Tim. 2:15.
[4] Cf., Eph. 5:17.

ples to evangelize people from all the nations, bringing them to Christ and assimilating them into Christianity.

But in point of fact, Jesus did not ask them to make converts! He asked them to make disciples. And these second generation disciples should not only learn the truth being passed on to them, but also observe it as they lived their own lives. Part of what they learned and needed to observe was the divine mandate to do exactly what the first-generation disciples of Jesus had done. They had gone out wherever the circumstances of life had led them, and they had made disciples. They had made disciples *by baptizing* the people who believed in Jesus and *by teaching* them so well that the new disciples understood how to observe or keep the commands that were being passed on to them.

All should teach then. But not all should seek formal teaching positions. Let the gifted in teaching fill the posts for teaching, remembering that a stricter judgment awaits them.

James was not simply trying to limit the number of teachers there might be within the Body of Christ over all or in any particular local church. He was trying to emphasize the difficulty and the repercussions that arise in every teaching ministry. As a result, the teaching ministry of a church should not be taken lightly because it is easy to cause the whole audience to stumble if they receive as truth the personal *assumptions* that the teacher has formulated without any *explicit* support from God's Word.

It is so very easy to misunderstand the Scriptures when they are not studied together as a whole. And when the teacher misunderstands them, he naturally misleads his disciples so that they repeat his errors.

For example, Matt. 18:19-20 are taken by many to be a prayer promise. Those verses say,

"Again I say to you, that if two or you agree on earth about *anything that they may ask*, it shall be done for them by My Father who is in heaven. For where two or three have gathered together in My name, there I am in their midst." (emphasis mine)

If two persons or a group of three individuals can get together and can agree on anything that they are praying about, they can be assured that Jesus is in their midst, hearing their prayers and that His heavenly Father will act to grant the requests for which they are praying. This is a long-standing view of these verses, one that has led many people to doubt God, the truthfulness of His Word, and their own faith. Why? Because so many prayers seem to remain unanswered.

As a very young Christian, I can remember being taught this interpretation by a well-respected Bible memory system. It assured me that these verses were a prayer promise, guaranteeing me the answer to all the prayers I prayed within that small prayer group. Then I heard the president of a seminary explain these verses in their immediate context.

I was completely surprised to learn that these verses have almost nothing to do with prayer *per se*. They were describing the assurance that those needed who were implementing church discipline upon a sinning, unrepentant member of their congregation. Jesus would be present to enable them in carrying out the discipline that was necessary.

In other words, if the process of church discipline had been carried out the way God had instructed them to do it, and if the decision that was reached was representative of God's own evaluation of the sin that had been committed, then Jesus would be present throughout the process and God the Father would carry out the spiritual aspects of the discipline in order to convict the unrepentant's heart fulfilling His purpose in the disci-

15

pline. The context is church discipline, not prayer *per se*.

Many Christians have experienced great heartache and confusion because God has not answered their prayers as this passage seems to suggest that He will (when it is interpreted wrongly). Their disappointment and frustration have become a considerable stumbling block to their own spiritual growth. Now they aren't sure how to take the Bible. They aren't certain that God really answers prayers as He promises to do. All of these doubts arise because those who used this passage to teach on prayer have misled these vulnerable folks.

There is an old hymn that corrects much of what is happening today. The name of that hymn is *Standing on the Promises*. That hymn used to be my favorite song growing up even before I knew much of anything that was actually taught in the Bible. The words of the second verse make the point that we ought to focus upon. It says:

> Standing on the promises that cannot fail,
> When the howling storms of doubt and fear assail,
> By the Living Word of God I shall prevail,
> Standing on the Promises of God.[1]

If we will stand on the *explicitly* stated truths of God's Word, and walk away from the *assumptions* of men that are so prevalent in our present-day theologies, we will be able to run the race that God has set before us in a way that will resemble the apostles of old. But as Joshua told the children of Israel, we must "choose for yourselves today whom you will serve."

Will we serve the *assumptions* of men or the *explicit* statements of God's Word? The choice is ours to make; but a stricter judgment comes upon the one who mishandles God's Word.

---

[1] Retrieved from http://library.timelesstruths.org/music/Standing_on_the_Promises/ on 3/31/15.

Chapter 2

The Misguided Spiritual Syllogism

Back in the early 90's, a movie came out starring Robert Redford, Sidney Poitier, Ben Kingsley, David Strathairn, and Dan Aykroyd. The name of the movie was *Sneakers*. A German mathematician had created a computer program that could virtually break any code used in the United States. Naturally everyone wanted it. The C.I.A. wanted it to break the codes and listen in to all the other government agencies. The mafia wanted it to keep their money laundering activities secret. Of course, all the foreign governments wanted it to break into America's systems.

Redford and his team manage to steal the code breaker from the German inventor who is subsequently murdered by the mafia. Redford then hands the program over to two men posing as agents from a secret branch of the American government. In reality they worked for the mafia and were sent to him from his good friend whom he had thought died in prison after a college prank twenty years earlier.

As Redford was stealing the program back from the mafia, his friend tried to talk him into staying and working with him in the mafia family. The future would be determined by those who could control the information that was disseminated around the world, the friend said. And with this program, this code breaker, one person could do control it all starting right now. Cos, Redford's college friend who had gone to prison for the prank they had pulled in school and who was now the mafia's administrator, summarized the principle upon which he thought life is based:

"Life is run not on reality but the perception of reality."

This axiom is the motivation behind much of the news that is distributed throughout America today. Most of the news that is given out by the different media sources seem to be almost scripted, duplicated, and then distributed by the various news channels. The decision-makers behind each major news network lead the viewers by the emphases and perspectives that they place on the news. This slant upon the news is presented to lead the viewer to reach the conclusion that they want him to reach. And since this slant is so widely reiterated by the various news channels, many simply believe what they hear on the news.

The media sources are trying to convince their audiences that their perception of reality is true. This is the reason that independent sources need to be accessed to confirm the stories being broadcast as well as the messages behind the stories.

The book of Proverbs has an appropriate observation for all of us today. It says,

"The first to plead his case *seems* just,
Until another comes and examines him." (Prov. 18:17)

Truth usually comes out on cross-examination. Without cross-examination, the viewer is limited to just the communication and perspective that others want to impress upon him.

There are some countries, like North Korea, whose government controls all the country's information. There isn't, I understand, any free, unrestricted communication with the outside world. Even access to the internet is severely restricted, and all radio and television information, originating within the country is screened. The facts that are taught in school are restricted to those the government approves, and only to those. Most outsiders who come from free societies typically call this sort of control brain washing.

While such control of communication venues and the messages that are broadcast over them are a travesty, we must understand that holding back information and even brain washing actually happens in all walks of life. And rather than being a rarity, such controlled communication occurs every day. Regardless of where I travel, whether it is to different parts of the United States of America or to other countries around the world, most of the people treat the information that repeatedly confronts them as *truth or fact*.

So, for example, if all one hears are the affirmations concerning the obvious benefits of organic foods and purified water, he chooses to buy organic foods and purified water without thinking further on the matter. He sees no need to test the ubiquitous praises since everyone around him has accepted them and surely, he thinks to himself, there ought to be far less harm in consuming them than their non-organic counterparts.

As one reads up on this matter on the internet, he quickly sees that it is not as cut and dried as many want to believe. In fact, apart from the scare tactics that are pervasive in this little battle, as it is in many other cultural battles as well, there are no facts that separate these two groups of foods by that much. As one pro-organic website admits,

> "But many experts say *there's not enough evidence to prove any real advantage to eating organic foods.* 'There's really very limited information in people on actual health outcomes with consumption of these products,' says David Klurfeld, PhD, chairman of the department of Nutrition and Food Science at Wayne State University in Detroit. *'We don't know enough to say that one is better*

than the other.'"[1]

On the other hand, the proponents rightly argue,

> "If you're talking about pesticides, the evidence is pretty conclusive. Your chances of getting pesticide residues are much less with organic food,' says John Reganold, professor of soil science at Washington State University in Pullman, Wash. Reganold points to a large-scale study done by the Consumers Union. Researchers looked at data from more than 94,000 food samples and 20 different crops. They found that organically grown crops consistently had about one-third as many pesticide residues as the conventionally grown versions. Organic foods also were far less likely to contain residues of more than one pesticide."

The quick but insufficient decision would be that the balance obviously sides with the organic foods. But this supposed expert goes on to say,

> *"'Even so, the amount of man-made pesticide residues found in conventional foods is still <u>well below</u> the level that the Environmental Protection Agency has deemed unsafe.* The real issue is whether these small doses, over years and decades, might add up to an increased health risk down the line. Is it going to make a difference? I don't know,' says Reganold. 'But it's something to think about, and we're the guinea pigs.'"*[2]* (emphasis mine)

So, whether you attribute the increase in consumption of organic foods and the designation of more and more land to the production of organic foods to the scare-the-hell-out-of-you fear tactics or to something else, people seem more convinced that organic foods are safer and better for you even without the usually demanded evidence. Spending more, sometimes a lot more, for the foods they want is assumed to be worth it health-wise.

I am certainly not a student of this cultural (not health) issue. But I have lived over 70 years eating only non-organic foods. The results of this debate, as far as I'm concerned, have been in a

---

[1] http://www.webmd.com/food-recipes/features/organic-food-better, p. 1.
[2] Ibid, p. 2.

long time ago. But the withholding of information and the brain washing, that the perpetual reiteration of one side of an issue creates, will continue as long as there is profit to be made.

The same phenomenon takes place within the religious realm. The same sound bites have been repeated over and over so often that there are few who would even think of challenging the traditional mind-set about, for example, forgiveness being related to believing in Jesus. Christian leaders have taught a syllogism for over five hundred years that, they say, summarizes the Christian faith with respect to this issue. It goes like this:

Believing in Jesus obtains forgiveness for sins.
Forgiveness of sins must be obtained to go to heaven.
Therefore, without believing in Jesus no one goes to heaven.

What understanding and faithful Christian would deny this syllogism? Its truthfulness is beyond any and all reproach, right? Well, that is one of the traditional tenets of orthodox Christianity that we want to test in this book. *Does the Bible actually propagate this syllogism, or has the syllogism been created to propagate a particular theological understanding?*

To my utter surprise I have found that it is the latter option rather than the former that explains the syllogism and its usage. For decades I used that syllogism thinking that I was following the Scriptures because I had been taught that I was. But was I really? I finally discovered that I was not.

The Scriptures versus the Syllogism

There are several facts that fly into the teeth of this syllogism. And the result? Rather than the facts being easily assimulated into the syllogism, the teeth of the syllogism are broken, chipped, and lost. Let's broach just a few of these facts to make my point.

21

First, as far as we know from the text of Scripture itself, there were righteous people in the OT who did not believe in Jesus nor in a coming Messiah-Savior. Even those who did believe in a coming Messiah, they never obtained their forgiveness through their faith in Him.

Second, when Moses wrote under the inspiration of the Spirit of God and declared that King Abimelech and the entire nation over which he was ruling at the time were righteous[1] before God, there had to have been some venue for them to experience forgiveness somewhere along the way. Yet, as far as we know from the *explicit* statements of Scripture, they were righteous and had obtained the forgiveness necessary to walk with God apart from trusting in a coming Messiah-Savior. Forgiven apart from faith in the coming Messiah? Is that possible? It seems all too clear that it is.

Third, the same forgiveness was obtained by Noah,[2] Job,[3] Abraham,[4] and Melchizedek.[5] All of these are *explicitly* declared to be righteous people in the Scriptures. But *never are we told* that before they were declared to be righteous, they had *explicitly* believed in Jesus or in a coming Messiah-Savior *for the forgiveness of the sins that they had committed.*

Fourth, another indication, that forgiveness of sins was not related to believing in a coming Messiah-Savior or in Jesus after He came upon the scene, presents itself when the sacrificial system that God introduced into the life of the Jewish people is correctly pondered. We can uncover this indication if we ask this

---

[1] Gen. 20:4, 5-6, 11.
[2] Gen. 6:8-9.
[3] Job. 1:6.
[4] Gen. 15:6; 17:1
[5] Gen. 14:18; Heb. 7:2.

22

question, "If the blood of bulls and goats could never take away sins, how is it that the nation of Israel was given a sacrificial ritual by which the sins of the individual as well as the sins of the nation were not only atoned for (covered) but also in the process of atonement were forgiven (taken away)?"

Repeatedly we encounter the reality of sins *being forgiven or taken away* in the OT as a result of obeying the guidelines of the sacrificial system. These sins were not just *covered*; they were *forgiven* as the Greek terms used in the Septuagint clearly establish. These are the same terms used in the NT for the forgiveness that Jesus' death provides. Yet, His death is *never called an atonement* in the NT although it provided for the forgiveness of sins.

We do not have the liberty of choosing which verses we follow and which verses we deny or ignore when they don't seem to fit into our theological grid. Since God cannot lie, His Word to man cannot contradict itself. Yet it is true that every interpreter is presented with a significant dilemma at this point. How can both concepts be true? How can the blood of bulls and goats not be efficacious to forgive sins[1] and yet sins were forgiven when the bulls and goats were sacrificed?[2]

While this dilemma is interesting and motivates us to seek a Scriptural solution, we must not lose sight of the point I'm trying to establish as I bring up this matter of harmony. And that point is this: *sins were forgiven in the OT apart from belief in Jesus or in a coming Messiah.* This was true both for the Jews who had the sacrificial system given to them by God and for the Gentiles who had to come to God apart from any divinely given sacrificial system.

---

[1] Heb. 10:1-4.
[2] Lev. 4:20, 26, 31, 35; 5:10, 13, 16, 18; 6:7; 19:22; etc.

The Jews had made a mistake in thinking that the Gentiles had to come to God through them. Christians today make the same mistake. They think that all the religions of the world have to come to God through them, or, at least, through faith in Jesus. *Coming to God* **through** *Jesus and coming to God* **by believing in** *Jesus are not the same thing in the Scriptures.* But, unfortunately, it is almost universally *assumed* to be synonymous.

The simplest way to harmonize the fact that forgiveness is taking place when the Jewish sacrificial system was properly obeyed, even though the blood of bulls and goats can never take away or remove (forgive) sins, is that the forgiveness came through the blood of Christ being applied rather than the blood of bulls and goats. Jesus was *foreknown* before the foundation of the world[1] and He was also *slain* at that time too.[2] Hence, God's grace, that provided for the forgiveness of sins in the death of Jesus, has been applying the work of the cross from the time of Adam and Eve forward, reaching all men in every age. The animal sacrifice was merely the condition that had to be met for the blood of Jesus to be applied. Through the blood of Christ forgiveness of sins was offered to anyone who was attempting to draw close to God and renew his fellowship with God for the purpose of serving Him.

God could designate *whatever means that pleased Him* to grant His forgiveness. Since mankind is spread out over the whole globe and since they live in very different cultures and have different amounts of revelation given to them, it is to be expected that different means would be used by God to grant His forgiveness for the different people groups. And this expectation is

---

[1] 1Pet. 1:17-21.
[2] Rev. 13:8.

exactly what we see in the Bible.

Some of the means that God required to grant His forgiveness are as follows:

Bringing a sacrifice (trusting in God to forgive)
Praying for forgiveness (trusting in God to forgive)
Touching hot coals to a prophet's lips (trusting God to forgive)
Repentance (trusting in God to forgive)
Baptism (trusting in God to forgive)
Confession of sins (trusting in God to forgive)

These and others will be expounded upon later in our study.

While outward obedience alone never accomplishes God's will nor pleases Him, the obedience that flows from faith always does.[1] But, interestingly enough, nowhere, that I am aware of, does *initially believing in Jesus* accomplish the same result as the other means listed above, namely, obtaining the forgiveness of sins.[2] After looking intently into the four Gospels, which constitute nearly half of the NT, I can say that *Jesus never offered forgiveness of sins to a person if he would place his faith in Him.* That *fact* is striking. Wouldn't we naturally expect an offer of forgiveness to be included in the invitation that Jesus gave to a person to believe in Him? That is what we've been taught, right?

The truth appears to be that *God has been applying the work of the cross to mankind **before** Jesus ever came and died.* Rather than God erupting in anger over man's sin and establishing an insurmountable chasm between man and Himself, He immediate-

---

[1] Heb. 11:6. Hebrews eleven refers mostly to men finding approval with God before the Law was given. This demonstrates that a relationship with God could exist apart from faith in a coming Messiah who, *supposedly*, was enigmatically portrayed in the sacrificial system outlined by the Law. Without the NT, it is a vague representation at best.
[2] There is a caveat here. When a person who had previously rejected Jesus trusts in Him, the sins connected with his former rejection are forgiven at that moment (Acts 2:37-41).

25

ly applied the work of the cross to their relationship so that He could maintain a communion with each person He had created. That is the love of God at work, a love that knows no bounds and is thwarted by no obstacle whatever, not even the sinfulness of man. It is always reaching out to man who may choose not to experience the overtures that God is making toward him. A life lived without divine communion is like a life lived in the smog of southern California!

Jesus' sacrifice removes (forgives) the sins committed by those who are pursuing a relationship with God. When they return, God is able to forgive their sins, and they are able to continue their walk with Him. As John the Baptist declared of Jesus, He is

> "the Lamb of God who *takes* (is taking or does take) *away* the sin of the world." (John 1:29)

Few Christians would question the fact that one of the reasons Jesus came to earth was to die to take away the sins that separate a man from intimate fellowship with God.

The old forensic paradigm, which became the standard view of the accomplishment of the death that Jesus died, has argued that Jesus' death paid the *eternal penalty of condemnation* resting upon man because of his sin. I once, and for a long time, believed that view of the death of Jesus, but not anymore. I simply can't find that *explicitly* stated in the Bible. In fact, I can't even find the *supposed* penalty of eternal condemnation for sin in the Scriptures. And, interestingly enough, no one has volunteered to show it to me. It is just *assumed* to be there somewhere.

Jesus died to remove or take away the sins that all men commit so that they can enter into fellowship with Him as they represent Him in all that they do. Consequently, these sins and the forgiveness needed for them have nothing whatever to do with a person's eternal destiny. The consequences of personal sins are restricted to this present life alone; they have nothing to do with the afterlife. Sins hinder a person's walk with God, not his reaching heaven for his eternal destiny.

We ought to notice from John the Baptist's comment that Jesus was the Lamb of God who *was presently taking away* the sins of the world. That is a fact of Scripture. And Jesus explicitly affirmed the fact that He had authority on earth to forgive sins.[1] But these facts ought to give us pause to consider how it can be true of those who have never even heard the name of Jesus.

Obviously, no one can believe in someone of whom they have never heard.[2] That is one of the reasons for the great commission: go and tell the world about Jesus! While we are to share Jesus with the world, it is not so they can be forgiven. They may already be experiencing a relationship with God because He has been forgiving them all the while they pursue Him. And their forgiveness has been provided *through* Jesus (but not *by believing in* Jesus).

The work of His death has been applied to all men throughout the history of mankind. The work of His resurrection has not been. The work of the resurrection is applied only to those who have believed in Jesus. We will discuss those results of the cross that have been applied to all men throughout history a little later in our study. We have already explained the results of the resurrection that are available only to those who believe in Jesus in previous volumes.

Since the death of Jesus deals with the sins of man, that is

---

[1] Mk. 2:10.
[2] Rom. 10:14-15; John 15:22-25.

one of the aspects of the cross that is applied to all. Having been slain before the foundation of the world,[1] the accomplishments of the death were ready to be applied right away, even to the first sin of Adam and Eve.[2] That is the reason that God came looking for our first parents after they had sinned: He was already reconciled to them and sought them out to be reconciled to Him by receiving His forgiveness if they returned to Him. God did not seek them out in anger. He was not holding a grudge against them because of their sin. He was pursuing them in love, grace, and mercy. That is the God of the Bible although it may not be the god our theologies have created.

In Noah, Job, Abraham, Melchizedek, Isaac, Jacob, Jacob's twelve sons, and even Moses who would become the great Law giver, we have examples of persons being forgiven without believing in Jesus. It was, nevertheless, true that by His death He provided what the Father needed to offer forgiveness to His wayward children. Ah, the grace of God! Ah, the love of God for every single person He has created, a love that provides His gracious forgiveness.

But don't be short-sighted. Forgiveness has never been God's end goal. Forgiveness has always been the means to an even more precious end: the experience of fellowship with God. That is what God is after. He created all men for the same purpose, namely, *to have fellowship with Him as they represent Him in all that they do.* That is God's goal in this life for every person.

Isn't it interesting that some persons are more greatly enticed by an eternal destiny than an intimate fellowship with the God of all life? No one can have what hasn't been offered. But it

---

[1] Rev. 13:8.
[2] Rom. 3:25.

stands to reason that what has been offered, since it was offered by the infinitely wise and immeasurably loving God, must be the very best thing that could ever be offered. Every person's life will change for the better when he decides to return to God, receive His unlimited forgiveness, and walk in His presence throughout the days that he has remaining in his life. Meaning, purpose, and extraordinary fulfillment result. Interested?

Chapter 3

Christ's Death and the Sacrificial System

In the opening scene of Walt Disney's version of *The Adventures of Peter Pan*, Peter is looking for his shadow which has become disconnected from him somehow. And as long as it was detached from him, it had no identity of its own. It could be anything; it could mean anything. It had no independent meaning of its own. It was just an empty, dark blotch without substance.

So, Peter chased it all over the room, waking up the children asleep in the room. He chased it up the side wall; he crawled after it on the ceiling overhead. When he finally caught it, he has Wendy, the oldest of all the siblings in the house, sow the shadow back in place at the side of his foot. No longer could the shadow be separated from the reality of which it was a general outline.

It is the common belief among Christians that the death of Christ fulfills in some way the sacrificial system of the OT. And that belief is exactly what Hebrews eight through ten seems to *explicitly* demand. For example, Heb. 10:1 says,

> "For the Law, since it has only **a shadow of the good things to come and not the very form of things**, can never by the same sacrifices year by year, which they offer continually, make perfect those who draw never." (emphasis mine)

Literarily we describe this phenomenon as a *type* being fulfilled by an *antitype*. The sacrificial system of the Mosaic Law is a *type* of the sacrifice that Jesus would offer when He came to earth. The Jewish ritualistic, sacrificial system is *the shadow cast back-*

ward into the OT by Christ's sacrifice, occurring over fourteen hundred years after God had given the sacrificial system to Israel. So, we either can work from the shadow toward the person (or event) casting the shadow, or we can work from the substance (the person or act) casting the shadow backward. But each is limited to and defined by the other. We will find that there is more to the reality than there is in the shadow, and that is to be expected.

But if everyone agrees that the death of Christ fulfills the sacrificial system in the OT or, to put it in the reverse way, if everyone agrees that the sacrificial system predicts what Jesus would accomplish in His death, why is there a need to broach this issue at all? Is there really any debate here?

The need arises because the *purpose* of the Law and the *results* for obeying it (or for disobeying it) are topics that are far from settled among religious leaders. Many Christians believe that the Law outlined for the Jews *the way of salvation.* By that phrase, they mean to affirm that obedience to the Law was the way to heaven in the OT. Hence, if a person obeyed the Law *perfectly* (that word is always slipped into the discussion somewhere), he would merit eternal life and thereby guarantee for himself a place in heaven. But if he disobeyed the Law, even in just one small instance, he would *supposedly* fail to meet God's standard for entrance into heaven. It was an all-or-nothing-at-all situation.

Not only does the Bible never tell us that obeying the Law perfectly is *a means of salvation* (i.e., using the term here in the way that traditional, Christian orthodoxy does to refer to going to heaven when a person dies), it likewise never tells us that disobeying the Law, even gross and protracted disobedience, results in an eternal sentence in the fires of hell. These ideas have been constructed by men in a sincere attempt to understand the overall message of the Bible. The problem is their construction does not fit the blueprints that the Bible actually draws up.

Not once does the Bible ever actually say that obedience to the Law of Moses, much less *perfect* obedience to it, is the condition for salvation (i.e., going to heaven). Not once is there any indication that heaven is lost by the disobedient, and hell is merited in its place. The Law was not given to save people from a *presumed* eternal condemnation which was *presumably* already resting upon them. It was not intended to lead the *lost person*, who is *presumed* to be eternally condemned, to an *initial faith* in God, which faith *presumably* saves him from hell and guarantees him a pass from judgment and a place in heaven with God forever. All of these *presumptions* must be brought to the Biblical text in order to find them in it.

Speaking practically and Biblically, the Law was never given as *a way of salvation* (i.e., of obtaining heaven). It was given as *a way of life*. It sets forth the lifestyle that God desired Israel to lead *until* He sent Israel's Messiah to her people.

And, it is just as important to note, the Mosaic Law was not binding upon the Gentile in any way unless that Gentile had become a proselyte to the Jewish faith. Rather, the Mosaic Law was the national charter for the Jewish nation. The Gentiles had another standard altogether to live by, but it too was from God![1] That standard was given through nature, or implanted within the conscience, or communicated in direct revelations from God Himself. But make no mistake about this: every Gentile nation

---

[1] Both Rom. 3:27-31 and 9:30-33 tell the reader plainly that the Gentile could live righteously before God without the Law that He had given to Israel.

33

has had a clear revelation from God so that they could know Him truly and walk with Him personally.

If you review the story of the Exodus, which immediately precedes the giving of the Law through Moses, you will easily find overwhelming evidence that the people liberated from Egypt were already considered God's own people. Consequently, we are forced to understand *the sacrifice of the Passover Lamb* as a protection for those who already belonged to God. Likewise, *the redemption from Egypt* (and *the purchase price* executed by God for that redemption) must be seen as a benefit done for those who had not only trusted in God already but who were following Him in the midst of these great trials. And finally, *the Law* was given to God's recently protected and redeemed people to guide them in living a life that pleased God without reference to the life hereafter.

Hence, no one was being *saved* in the traditional sense of orthodox Christianity. The people involved in the Passover and in the Exodus and who were described as being redeemed and being bought in these events, were those who belonged to God already. *These things happened to them because of their continuing faith in God.*

But if a person reads the Exodus story and tries to fit it into an eternal-redemption-from-hell template, the straightforward physical redemption of Israel from Egypt will be recast, ignoring the historical situation and elevating a spiritual interpretation of redemption from hell in its place. Forcing the story of the Exodus into a Christian, theological grid of spiritual redemption *distorts the historical event and redefines the terms used to describe it.* And once it is done there, it will be hard not to use that same approach later on when the Scriptures are being interpreted.

34

Once literal interpretation is cast aside, all meaning comes from the interpreter rather than from the original writer of Scripture.

If the *Passover* was a memorial feast to commemorate God's protection of *people who already belonged to Him*, and if the *Redemption* spoken of describes the physical deliverance of *people who already belonged to Him*, and if the *Exodus* was undertaken by *people who already belonged to Him*, then the sins that are being forgiven through *the sacrificial system* of the Jewish people are those of *people who already belong to Him*. The "unbeliever's" sins are never addressed in the sacrificial system given to the Jewish people. Rather, what is clearly set before the reader is the *continuing faith* of the descendants of Abraham who were about to become a nation. As such they would be organized under a legal charter given by God to guide the nation in the service He wanted from them.

If Jesus fulfills the sacrificial system as most Christians suppose, then we must conclude that He died for those who already have a relationship with God, or, as we have generally described it in the past, He died for those we call *believers* in contradistinction to those we call *unbelievers* (but that is another theological *presumption* which redefines both words in terms of each group's *presumed* eternal destiny). The term *believer* in the Scriptures is simply describing a person who has believed God for something in the past, or who is believing God for something in the present, or who should begin believing God for something in his immediate future (i.e., in his next breath) or in his distant future. An *unbeliever* is someone who is not believing God for something that he should be. *Neither term is designed to say anything about the person's eternal destiny.* But both terms focus entirely upon the present state of a person's heart. Hence, an unbeliever may presently become a believer and then return to function as an unbeliever again. Likewise, the believer may presently turn away from God and become an unbeliever and then return to his former way of life and begin believing in God again. In short, these terms are not used for groups which are static and unchangeable.

All men have some kind of relationship with God because He made them all for that purpose. He created all men to have communion with Him (that is the reason He made them in His image). Jesus died so that all men could walk with God wherever they live regardless of the influences of the culture in which they live. God expects a man's faith response to His revelation to them to overcome the cultural limitations and errant perspectives[1] that exist around him and the deceptions and distortions arising from indwelling sin[2] within him. The cross, being applied by God to all men throughout the history of mankind, has made this spiritual walk possible for all men. As a result, all men can pursue God and fulfill the original purpose for which God had created them: *to have fellowship or communion with God while they represented Him in all that they do.*

So, Jesus died for all men throughout the whole world, beginning with Adam and Eve, extending from Cain and Seth to all of their descendants. But some of the results of that death are conditional and some are unconditional; some of the results are applied without man responding at all in any way while other results require man to pursue God by faith. We will cover these results now briefly.

---

[1] Cf., 1Cor. 8:7.
[2] Rom. 7:11; Heb. 3:12-13.

Indwelling sin was overcome for all men universally without anyone having to fulfill any condition such as pursuing a relationship with God by faith. Nevertheless, indwelling sin will naturally reign within the life of each person if he does not pursue a relationship with God by faith. Victory over indwelling sin has been won at the cross but the fruit of it may not be experienced in the life of the believer if he chooses not to follow God's revelations to him.

On the other hand, having personal sins forgiven and spiritual death removed are wholly dependent upon a person seeking after God by faith. There is no forgiveness of sins for a person as long as he remains rebellious or indifferent to God. As long as he lives independently of God, he commits sin[1] and experiences spiritual death.[2] This is true of all, even of Christians. But spiritual death only means that a person is living by indwelling sin rather than by faith. Since the cross conquered indwelling sin, man has always had the choice to follow sin or to follow God's voice, however that voice may come to him.

So, generally speaking and in a summarizing overview, we can say that *the accomplishments of Jesus's death are being experienced only by those who are seeking after God*. His death was for *believers*, not in the restricted and inadequate sense of a heaven bound person, but rather in the sense of a person who is presently relying upon God as he carries out the instructions that God has given to him.

On the other hand, it naturally follows that the accomplishments of Jesus' death are not being experienced by *unbelievers*, that is, by those who are presently not relying upon God as they

---

[1] Rom. 14:23.
[2] Rom. 6:15-23; Eph. 2:1-3.

live their lives. Just as the sacrifices of the Jewish system were for the *believer* who cared about his relationship with God, so also Jesus' sacrificial death is for the person who cares about maintaining his relationship with God. He didn't die to bring lost sheep into the fold (the old paradigm); He died to protect and care for the sheep already in the fold (new paradigm). And all men are in the fold.[1] What they experience is limited to what truth God has revealed to them. If they are following the truth that God has revealed to them, and if they are relying upon God to sustain them and intervene in their obedience to make it successful, they are being cared for and are being protected by the God who has loved them from the beginning.

Add to this the conclusions from volume one of this series, The Prodigal Paradigm. 1.) No mention of initial faith ever. Hence, the Bible is not about the lost (in terms of our traditional but errant orthodox teaching meaning bound for hell) being found; 2.) no mention of any other kind of forgiveness than filial. Forensic forgiveness is a matter of man's creation along with the forensic justification that was first formulated during the Reformation. When we put all this together, we realize that there is a great need to do a lot of rethinking. May God help us in that process.

---

[1] Cf., Ps. 24:1.

Chapter 4

Pictures of the Work of the Cross

As we meditate on the pictures of the cross that the Bible sets before us, I want you to think of these pictures as the border to a big puzzle. The border frames the picture and requires the rest of the puzzle pieces to fit inside of it. While the pictures I offer in this chapter are by no means all of the pictures that can be suggested, they are sufficient to limit and define the concepts that will go inside of the border that the Bible creates for the death of Christ.

We are fortunate to have some pictures given to us to help us discern the meaning of the death of Christ. These portraits do not lend themselves to the old forensic paradigm however. They don't promote the idea that *an eternal penalty* rests upon man for the sins that he has committed. Neither do they promote the idea that a person's *status* or *standing* before God is taken care of by the death Christ dies. There is no reason to believe that Christ's death seals a person's future in the afterlife, or that the forgiveness that His death provides has anything to do with eternity at all.

These portraits will aid us in reevaluating the forensic paradigm of an angry God who sits in judgment over all humans, giving a guilty verdict to each person who has not believed in Jesus (because he can't believe without God giving him the faith that he needs to do so) and a verdict of pardon to all those who have believed in Jesus (because of God's sovereign work to enable him to believe). Is that really what you see in the Scriptures?

Or has that been the explanation placed upon some general comments that could be taken in a variety of ways? The following portraits guide us to a different conclusion altogether.

Forsaken by the Father

The first picture that is snapped of the cross shows us that a separation was felt to have occurred between Jesus and the Father during the time when He was bearing the sins of all mankind. Sometime after that feeling of separation occurred, Jesus cried out,

"My God, My God, why have You forsaken Me?" (Matt. 27:46)

The word used here is a compound Greek term which refers to a desertion, to leaving a person completely, to walking away from him or forsaking him. We can't know more than what God has given us to know. Did God desert Jesus? Did He walk away from Him and leave Him on His own? Or was this simply the feeling that came over Jesus in His humanity? If Jesus promises never to forsake or leave His children, it is probable that He didn't actually forsake or leave Jesus, His unique Son. But it still could feel that way.

This is a love story, not a court case! Jesus bore the sins of the world and as a consequence felt separated from the Father's love and care. If this is the only penalty resting upon the sins that Jesus bore for mankind, it is plain that the penalty resting upon sin has nothing to do with eternity or with some supposed sentence to hell. And notice carefully that there is no mention of God's wrath in connection to Jesus' death much less in His experience after He died.

Whatever the penalty was, Jesus bore it *before* He died as is indicated by His cry, "Why have you forsaken Me?" And there is no indication that either this forsaking continued *after* He died or that another, even more severe penalty was placed upon Him later. This feeling of being forsaken by the Father during man's earthly life after having sinned is what Jesus died to prevent. There is nothing more to the proper interpretation of the death of Christ than that, at least as far as this snap shot of the meaning of the cross is concerned. The question is, Do the Scriptures *force* us to expand the picture that we get here?

It is natural to conclude therefore that Jesus' death dealt with and solved the dilemma of man's feeling separated from the Father, a separation from fellowship, intimacy, care, protection, and blessings. *This separation is what the Bible calls spiritual death.* But based upon Heb. 13:5 and Ps. 22:24, it is probable that Jesus only had a feeling of what this separation was like, rather than a real separation.[1]

This forsaking, this death, *is* the penalty or the consequence of each and every sin a person commits premeditatively. There is no further penalty that extends beyond this immediate consequence of spiritual separation from the Father's fellowship and blessings. The consequences of sin that Jesus dealt with and solved were temporal, having to do with this earthly life alone. His death provided solutions to every hindrance to a person's walk with God. As far as we know from the text that is before us, Jesus did not deal with eternal penalties that are *presumed* to be resting upon man's sins. He dealt with the feeling that man has after he has sinned, a feeling reflecting a real separation.

---

[1] I have to give credit to Paul Tiefel for suggesting this idea in my Thursday Bible study. He first related verse 24 to verse one of Ps. 22.

A Torn Veil

The next picture we have of the cross of Jesus Christ is the one of a torn veil in the Temple. At the moment of Jesus' death, the veil that separated the Holy Place from the Holy of Holies (or Most Holy Place) was torn in two from top to bottom.[1] Jewish tradition tells us that this veil was a tightly woven fabric two inches thick. To tear such a piece of cloth would be an extraordinary feat if not miraculous altogether. As with the other signs surrounding the death of Christ, this one too was produced by God alone.

The veil closed off any approach into the presence of God except for one person, the High Priest, on one particular day, the Day of Atonement. This day was a special time of personal soul searching for each Israelite.[2] Each person was called upon to survey his own life to see if there was any sin in his life that he had not taken care of by the prescribed sacrifices and by fulfilling the laws that further regulated the means to obtain forgiveness from God. But all of this soul searching was to make sure that God renewed His contract with Israel to use them as His *national agent* in the world for another year. This was a year-by-year contract with God. At any time it could be broken by non-compliance.

There was no sin being dealt with in this prescribed day of sacrifice that carried *an eternal penalty of consignment to hell*. No forgiveness being sought dealt with any other matter than being able to have fellowship with God as he represented Him in all that he did. The only consequence that Israel had to be afraid of experiencing was God's removal of her role as His primary, *na-*

---

[1] Matt. 27:51.
[2] Lev. 16:29-34; 23:26-32.

tional agent in the world, a world that needed spokesmen for God and representatives of Him because so many had gone astray.

Jesus died on the day of Passover, a feast day that commemorated Israel's deliverance from the bondage they were under in the land of Egypt. This day was a day of *redemption*;[1] it was a day of *being purchased*[2] by the awesome God who had displayed His greatness in the ten plagues that He brought upon the land of Egypt to free His people. Not only was each plague against a different god of Egypt, together they were intended to lead the Egyptians to understand that Israel's God was the one true God.

Again, there was no sin being dealt with in this prescribed day of sacrifice that carried an eternal penalty of consignment to hell. In fact, like the ceremony prescribed on the Day of Atonement, the ceremonies for the Feast of Passover and of Unleavened Bread focus wholly upon each person's relationship with God. Worshipping God without the presence of conscious sin in one's life was one of the goals of all of Israel's feasts and prescribed holy days. None of them dealt with some *presumed* eternal consequence which was supposedly placed upon their sin. All of these feasts and holy days focused upon maintaining the relationship between God and the participant; they were not concerned with establishing a new relationship with God, one that had not previously existed between God and the participant. To use the language of our day and the concepts with which most are familiar, none of the feasts were *evangelistic*; none had the purpose of *"saving the lost"* (terms that are almost universally misunderstood today).

---

[1] Ex. 15:13. The meaning of this redemption is further explained in Ex. 13:11-16 without giving any possibility for attaching eternal consequences to the rite.
[2] Ex. 15:16.

So, in keeping with that focus, when the veil of the Temple was torn in two, that torn veil symbolized that Jesus' death provided a way into God's presence for all who wanted to go. Only the High Priest could enter into the Most Holy Place, in which a particular form of God's presence resided over the mercy seat, and he could do that only once a year. Through Christ's death every person, Jew and Gentile alike, could enter into God presence all day, every day, to maintain a personal relationship with Him. A more profound change can't be imagined.

Christ's death had nothing to do with removing some *supposed* eternal penalty of condemnation from the person who trusted in Jesus. It rather provided a way for every man to come into the Father's presence while he still lived upon the earth.[1] He didn't need to be a High Priest to come into His presence, and he didn't have to wait to come only on a certain prescribed day once a year. He could now come into God's presence and reside there as long as he liked. Just like Mary who chose to sit at the feet of Jesus, every man today can choose to enter into the presence of the Father and stay there, having communion with Him in much the same fashion as Mary did with Jesus.[2]

The sacrificial system was given to Israel to tutor them,[3] preparing the nation, as well as all who would study its system, to grasp what the coming Messiah would be like and what He would accomplish in His death for the world. While His death had already occurred before the foundation of the world so that it could be applied readily to all men throughout the whole world,[4] it still needed some type of portrayal to each generation

---

[1] John 14:6.
[2] Lk. 10:38-42.
[3] Gal. 3:21-24.
[4] 1Pet. 1:17-21; Rev. 13:8; Rom. 3:25.

so that the meaning would not be lost or a new meaning be put in place of God's intended meaning.

In summary, the sacrificial system was intended to instruct all people on the needs that they had and how the Messiah would satisfy those needs before God. The sins that would separate each man from personal fellowship with God would be taken care of in the cross of Jesus so that each man could reenter God's presence, regardless of what he had done after leaving His presence, and return to an intimate relationship with the Father. None of the sacrifices dealt with any *supposed eternal penalty* that rested upon man for his sins. None of the sacrifices offered a forgiveness that gained heaven and by-passed hell. And as it was explained in the previous chapter, the sacrificial system was the *shadow* of the coming *reality*. It prepared us to understand the significance of Christ's death for sins.

The Good Shepherd

John ten probably has as much about the death of Christ, coming directly from the Lord Himself, as any passage in the whole NT. As He spoke of His coming death in the context of His extended metaphor of a shepherd and his sheep, He emphasized several truths which ought to form a third side of the border for our puzzle on the death of Christ. Jesus distinguishes between the good shepherds and the hirelings in the first part of the chapter. He explained that there were four things that distinguished the shepherd: 1.) he is recognized by the gate-keeper; 2.) *his* sheep respond to his voice; 3.) he calls his own sheep by name; 4.) he leads his sheep out of the pen into pasture.[1] All of these things focus upon the shepherd's reputation and his care

---

[1] John 10:3.

for his flock.

The most significant contributions that John ten makes help define and give a proper understanding to the death of Christ, salvation, and eternal life, three of the most important concepts in the NT. The point of being *saved* is the promise of being led out of the fold *to find pasture*.[1] Salvation, then, is described in terms of *feeding* God's sheep. But in order to explain exactly what finding pasture is (or what feeding His sheep is), Jesus carefully explained that it had to do with a life He wanted to give to all who believe in Him. In addition, He connected the idea of going in and out to find pasture to feed upon daily to His purpose for coming. He said,

> "I came that you might have **life** and have it **abundantly**." (John 10:10b, emphases mine)

To find pasture is to experientially have life abundantly. Or, in other familiar terms, it is a reference *to being given eternal life moment by moment* as a person, represented here as a sheep, follows Jesus, the good Shepherd.[2] Here eternal life is described as a repetitive inflow of life from the Son, whose life it is, to the sheep that He desires to feed.

These are two concepts here. Eternal life is given upon initial faith in Jesus as the Messiah sent from God.[3] At that moment the believer has *access* to the eternal life that has been given,[4] but *he does not necessarily experience the life that he possesses*.[5] To experience the life that he now possesses he must live by faith, trusting the Spirit of God to give life (or to infuse Christ's eternal life)

---

[1] John 10:9.
[2] John 10:27-29.
[3] John 6:47, 68-69; 20:31.
[4] Cf., Rom. 5:1-2; 2Pet. 1:3-4; Lk. 15:29-31.
[5] Rom. 6:15-23, esp. vv. 16, 23.

into his constitution.[1] Being in possession of eternal life means that he has access into God's grace for living abundantly.[2] But if he doesn't use that access and actually tap into that life, it remains *a life within that is never appropriated or lived*.

What does all this have to do with the death of Christ Jesus? It explains that *the death of Christ was for the life of His sheep*. He did not die for them to remove some *presumed* eternal penalty that was resting upon them. They were not doomed for the slaughter house of hell because they had sinned. *The penalty for their sin was the death that they were currently experiencing[3] as they walk by the power of indwelling sin.*[4] Jesus died to open a way into the presence of the Father that would spiritually nourish them, and through that nourishment protect them from the wolves that were seeking to take their (spiritual) life from them.

Lastly, while we will devote a whole chapter to defend this view later in the book, I want to suggest that the good Shepherd doesn't die *vicariously* for His sheep. That is, *He doesn't die in their place*. He is not *substituted* for them. Unlike the hireling who runs away when the wolves approach, the Good Shepherd dies to keep the wolves from ravishing the sheep. Just as the Passover Lamb was slain for the protection of the Israelites, so the Good Shepherd dies for the protection of His sheep. In both cases (His) death is for the temporal protection of His sheep. In neither case was the matter of heaven or hell involved. Their *redemption* was from the affliction that they faced in their lives.

---

[1] Eph. 3:16-17; Gal. 2:20.
[2] Cf., Rom. 5:1-2; 2Tim. 2:1.
[3] Rom. 6:23.
[4] Rom. 6:12-13, 16; 8:6.

The Mercy Seat

This fourth side may be the most emotionally moving part of the border that we see presented to us in the NT. Most students of the Bible are familiar with *the mercy seat on top of the Ark of the Covenant* that stood in the Most Holy Place in the Tabernacle and later in the Temple built by Solomon. Once a year the High Priest entered this room through the veil that separated the Most Holy Place from the Holy Place in which the altar of incense, the table of consecrated bread, and the menorah stood. He entered the room to bring in the blood of a sacrifice and sprinkle it upon and before the Mercy Seat so that God would forgive all the sins that the nation of Israel had committed during the previous year, retaining them as His *national* servants for another year.

There was no provision made to clean the blood off of the Mercy Seat once it had been sprinkled upon it. So, year after year, the blood would accumulate until the day came when the last sacrifice would be given, providing a perpetual Mercy Seat at which God would meet with any man who wanted to come into His presence to commune with Him.

Paul says in Rom. 3:25 that God appointed Jesus as that Mercy Seat. While most Bibles translate the term Paul uses here as propitiation, yet the OT's use of that term strongly argues against that notion. The Septuagint's (LXX) use of that term as a name for the Mercy Seat makes it unlikely that Paul had in mind the idea of a propitiation.[1] As the text explicitly says, Jesus functions as God's Mercy Seat *through the faith* a person exercises in order to come before God.[2] The propitiation that Jesus offered to

---

[1] Zane Hodges, *Romans*, p. 100.

[2] Ibid. While Hodges sees this as a once for all operation of the Mercy Seat, I take it to be continuous in nature, occurring over and over as often as a person needs to deal with his sins.

God for man's sins was efficacious in and of itself. Each man's faith in Jesus was not needed for the payment to God to be applied to him.

There are several reasons that suggest that Paul meant to set forth Jesus' death as providing a *continuing* Mercy Seat between God and man rather than one that is used one time at initial faith in Jesus. Some of these reasons are as follows: 1.) Paul was contrasting Gentile and Jewish *"believers"* throughout his entire argument in his letter to the Romans; 2.) Paul's concept of justification is not a once-for-all declaration by God since he chose to use Abraham as his model for it; 3.) The Mercy Seat was never approached on behalf of the so-called *"unbeliever;"* 4.) And the Mercy Seat was never approached one time on behalf of anyone; it was a yearly event and, therefore, repetitive in the nature of the case.

The point is that both justification and Jesus' functioning as a Mercy Seat are corollary concepts that occur over and over again throughout a person's life. And Jesus' death makes both possible if only one will walk by faith. So, neither justification nor the use of the Mercy Seat takes place only one time, and neither has anything to do with a person's eternal destiny. In His blood there is redemption by which He purchases back the person who has strayed into bondage once again, and by that same blood He becomes the Mercy Seat for the repentant returning to God whether from a distant country or from a distant heart living at home.

We ought to allow these four pictures of Christ's death to form the borders around the rest of the information the NT gives us about His death. If we will do that, we will realize that all of the accomplishments of the death of Christ have to do with living life.

He died that we might come before the Father as our sins are taken away and fellowship with God is restored.

He died so that no man has to feel forsaken by the Father because of the sins that he commits, both consciously and unconsciously.

He died so that all men can enter into God's present whenever they return to Him to reinstitute and revitalize the relationship between them.

He died so that the wolves may not ravage them due to the life that He grants to them moment by moment.

He died to be the Mercy Seat for anyone who is returning to God or trying to maintain a relationship with Him.

That last one happens to be my personal favorite. No fear! No shame! Only mercy when we return! What grace!

Chapter 5

Atonement versus Forgiveness

Over forty years ago I heard an illustration of the difference between the terms used for atoning (or atonement) and those used for forgiving (and forgiveness). I was asked to think about my last Thanksgiving dinner. In the South that meal would generally include turkey, dressing, green bean casserole, mash potatoes, cream gravy, brown gravy, sweet potatoes with a brown sugar and pecan glaze, cranberry sauce, honey baked ham, a typical green salad, rolls, corn bread, and, of course, iced tea. For dessert we would have an assortment of pies and cakes and homemade ice cream. Thanksgiving dinner was a big deal even for a family of modest means like mine was.

Then the speaker suggested that one of the children at the table dribbled some of the brown gravy on the white tablecloth as he poured the gravy from the gravy bowl. The closest adult quickly *covered up* those ugly brown spots by laying an extra napkin over them. The spots were, of course, still there; but they were hidden from sight. Later the hostess would wash that tablecloth *to remove* the spots permanently. That, the speaker suggested, is the difference between atonement and forgiveness. In atonement sins, the ugly spots, are *covered*, but in forgiveness sins are cleansed or *taken away* permanently. While that may not be precise, it is a very good starting point.

There are two facts of Scripture that must be understood and harmonized. On the one hand, the Bible is clear that the blood of bulls and goats can never take away (forgive) sins.[1] The writer of the Book of Hebrews says it this way:

> "For the Law . . . can never by the same sacrifices year by year, which they offer continually, make perfect those who draw near. . . . For *it is impossible for the blood of bulls and goats to take away sins.*" (Heb. 10:1-4, emphasis mine)

To take away sins removes them (or forgives them). The blood of bulls and goats cannot result in forgiveness. Yet, we find over and over in the OT that *when atonement is performed, forgiveness is given*. Note a couple of representative passages on this problem:

> "He shall also do *with the bull* just as he did with the bull of the sin offering; and thus he shall do with it. So the priest shall *make atonement* for them, and *they will be forgiven.*" (Lev. 4:20)

> "All its fat he shall offer up in smoke on the altar as in the case of the fat of the sacrifice of peace offerings. Thus the priest shall *make atonement* for him *in regard to his sin*, and *he will be forgiven.*" (Lev. 4:26)

> "Then he shall remove all its fat, just as the fat of the lamb is removed from the sacrifice of the peace offerings, and the priest shall offer them up in smoke on the altar, on the offerings by fire to the Lord. Thus the priest shall *make atonement* for *in regard to his sin* which he has committed, and *he will be forgiven.*" (Lev. 4:35)

> "So the priest shall *make atonement* on *his behalf* for his sin which he has committed, and *it will be forgiven* him." (Lev. 5:10)

> "The priest shall then *made atonement* for him *with the ram* of the guilt offering, and *it will be forgiven* him." (Lev. 5:16)

---

[1] I am suggesting that *forgiveness* is the same thing as sins *being taken away*, and that the Hebrew term used for *atonement* in the Bible doesn't have any connotations of *forgiveness* even though most resources suggest that it can mean forgiveness at times. My position is based upon the Book of Leviticus and the Book of Hebrews which seem to demand separate ideas. Also, the assumption that *to take away* and *to forgive* are synonymous is based upon the fact that unlike the animal sacrifices, Christ's sacrifice can *take away sins* (Heb. 10:4, 11) which act is described as *forgiveness* in Heb. 10:18.

"So the priest shall *make atonement* for him *concerning his error* in which *he sinned unintentionally* and did not know it, and *it will be forgiven* him." (Lev. 5:18)

"and the priest shall *make atonement* for him before the Lord, and *he will be forgiven* for any one of the things which he may have *done to incur guilt.*" (Lev. 6:7)

"The priest shall also *make atonement* for him with the ram of the *guilt offering* before the Lord for his sin which he has committed, and *the sin* which he has committed *will be forgiven* him." (19:22)

The priest offered the appropriate sacrifice in each case resulting in the *atonement* of the sins committed by the one bringing the sacrifice. But it is also clear that *forgiveness* is distinguished from the atonement achieved even though it accompanied the atonement in each case. There wasn't just the *covering* of sins; the *removal* of sins also occurred. And both of these were available only for sins that were *not premeditated* but were *unintentional*. For premeditated sins there was no sacrifice at all. If those sins were forgiven, the basis for that forgiveness was grace alone apart from any response that might be set by God as a condition for His grace to be given. To Israel's relief God established a Day of Atonement in which all of the sins that Israel had committed during the past year could be not only covered but also forgiven. With a clean slate each person could, with a clear conscience, once again pursue fellowship with God. And the nation could be confident in its continued role as God's *national* agent.

Christ's death is never called an atonement. It is a mystery why Christian theologians have debated the issue of whether Christ's atonement was limited or unlimited when it is never referred to as an atonement in the first place. The reason that Jesus' death is never called an atonement, of course, is that it was never meant

53

to *cover* the sins that had been committed; it was meant to *take them away, to remove them entirely.* Jesus' death is God's final response in dealing with man's sins. Once His sacrifice had been given, there would be no need for another.[1]

Sins could continue to be overlooked (or passed over) for anyone who had never heard of Jesus or who had rejected Him as Messiah when he had heard about Him. And when they were thus *atoned for* by whatever means God may have required, they would be removed forever through God's application of Jesus' death on the cross for those sins. So, if a Jew today were to pray to God (or to the place where the Temple once stood?[2]) for the forgiveness of his sins, or for any number of other things, God will hear from heaven and forgive his sins by applying the death of Jesus to them. *No one needs to know the reason why God forgives in order to obtain forgiveness from Him.* All forgiveness throughout the history of the world is given because of the sufficiency of Jesus' death for sins. But that fact may be unknown to many.

God made a provision to cover, or to atone for, sins temporarily for a variety of reasons such as, 1.) to train His people to take sin seriously and do what was needed to remove it as a barrier to fellowship with God; 2.) to teach His people what the Messiah must do when He finally came upon the scene so that they would receive Him when He offered Himself as that provision; 3.) to teach His people that while forgiveness is freely provided, it still must be sought in the ways that God designates.

God has ordained several different means through which He has granted the forgiveness of sins. For example, forgiveness was obtained in the Bible by obeying the sacrificial system,[3] by

---

[1] Heb. 10:18.
[2] See 1Kgs. 8:12-53.
[3] See the verses from *Leviticus* quoted earlier in this chapter.

having a hot coal pressed to your lips,[1] by repentance alone,[2] by water baptism if it is undertaken with a repentant heart,[3] by forgiving others,[4] by praying to God for it,[5] and by confession.[6] But we must be clear: forgiveness was *received* through these means, but none of those means could have resulted in forgiveness if God was not already offering it in these ways. *Through the cross alone* God provided for the forgiveness of all men's sins. Having been satisfied by Jesus' sacrifice for sins,[7] He could determine what means He would accept to give what He was offering.

If we focus upon the passages in Leviticus and in Hebrews chapter ten, several facts seem clear. These facts press for a distinction to be made between atonement and forgiveness.[8]

> **Atonement** is achieved through ritual, by the offering of sacrifices required for just that purpose.
> **Forgiveness**, on the other hand, is not based on ritual.
> **Atonement** is achieved by a man (in this case a priest).
> **Forgiveness** is not said to come from a man regardless of his religious status; it comes from God.
> **Atonement** through the blood of bulls and goats does not take away a person's sins (Heb. 10:1-4).
> **Forgiveness** through Christ Jesus' sacrifice takes away (forgives) sins (Heb. 10:11-12, 18).

If the animal sacrifices which the priest offered for the person bringing the sacrifice to make atonement could also effect forgiveness of sins, then Jesus would not have needed to come to

---

[1] Isa. 6:6-7.
[2] Lk. 17:4-5.
[3] Mk. 1:4; Acts 2:38.
[4] Matt. 6:14-15.
[5] 1Kgs. 8:12-53; Matt. 6:9-13.
[6] 1John 1:9.
[7] Cf., 1John 2:1-2; 4:10.
[8] Having reviewed all the instances in which the Hebrew verb *to atone for* is translated *forgive*, I see no contextual reason to accept the translation *forgive* in those instances.

die. That seems to be the conclusion reached by the author of the Book of Hebrews when he said,

> "Now where there is forgiveness of these things, there is no longer any offering for sin." (Heb. 10:18)

If any act of man could bring about forgiveness of sins, then God would not have had to send His Son to die. Jesus' death was *not* to make atonement; it was to provide a redemptive price[1] so that God was free to forgive mankind's sins, receive him back into His fellowship, and deliver him from his present enslavements.

In the OT, God granted forgiveness of sins so that fellowship could resume, not because the man's animal sacrifice merited it. He offered forgiveness of sins because man's obedience to the sacrificial rituals, demanded of him in the Law of Moses, fulfilled the condition that God had ordained for that forgiveness. God is a forgiving God by nature.[2] Consequently, He sent Jesus to earth so that He would die in order that the obstacle of personal sins could be taken out of the way, freeing Him to express His forgiving nature after atonement was achieved by man. God is not *waiting* for a sacrifice today to forgive. Rather, He is *seeking* spiritual worshippers returning to Him in truth.[3]

---

[1] Rom. 3:25; Eph. 1:7; 1Cor. 6:19-20.
[2] Ex. 34:6-7.
[3] John 4:23-24.

Chapter 6

Christ Died for the Whole World

It is a common feature of seminary study to delve into the debate over *the extent of the atonement.* Since, as I stated in the last chapter, *Christ's death is never referred to as an atonement,* there seems to be confusion in the study of Christ's death from the very beginning. Most theologians simply ignore this fact and write *as though* Christ's death is commonly referred to as an atonement or that atonement is an exact synonym for what takes place in His death.[1] But when Christ's death is called by a term that the Bible never uses for it, it is no longer a Biblical debate at all. It has become a duel of men's intellects rather than a discovery of God's revealed truth. And in this scenario, the smartest, most charismatic communicator wins the day although he may not have so much as a glimpse of God's truth in his arguments.

When the Bible clearly says that Christ died for the world, that must be the extent to which the accomplishments of the cross are applied by God. Some of the references establishing the fact that God's intention for the cross was universal include the following:

"Behold the Lamb of God who takes away *the sin of the world!"* (John 1:29)

---

[1] E.g., in *Recovering the Scandal of the Cross,* Baker and Green say, "Evidently, if we are to gain our bearings regarding the meaning of the atonement in the New Testament, we will be *less interested in the appearance of particular vocabulary* and more concerned with the concept of 'atonement,' which we will define broadly as 'the saving significance of Jesus' death.'" (pp. 52-3, of their second edition).

"and they were saying to the woman, 'It is no longer because of what you said that we believe, for we have heard for ourselves and know that this One is indeed *the Savior of the world.'*" (John 4:42)

"For the bread of God is He who comes down out of heaven, and *gives life to the world.*" (John 6:33, marginal reading)

"I am the living bread that came down out of heaven; if anyone eats of this bread, he shall live forever; and the bread also which I shall give for *the life of the world* is My flesh." (John 6:51)

"I am *the Light of the world*; he who follows Me shall not walk in the darkness, but shall have the light of life." (John 8:12)

"And if anyone hears My sayings, and does not keep them, I do not judge him; for I did not come to judge the world, but *to save the world.*" (John 12:47)

"And we have beheld and bear witness that the Father has sent the Son to be *the Savior of the world.*" (1John 4:14)

Other passages could easily be added to these,[1] but the point is established: *Israel's Messiah came to save the whole world through the cross.* Jesus plainly said, "*I came to save the world.*"[2] Since there are different *salvations*, as I have already explained in this series, the context alone will determine which is in view. But with respect to the cross it can be said that *whatever the cross accomplished, it accomplished those things for the whole world.*

Part of the reason for the continuing debate over identifying those for whom Jesus died is the fact there are passages that limit Christ's death to *many* or to *some*. So, one side leans on the verses that clearly say that the Christ died for *all*, and the other side leans on the verses that say Christ died for *some* or for *many*.

Both sides use the Bible to make their case. And both sides have ways to *explain away* the verses that seem to directly con-

---

[1] Especially, 2Cor. 5:18-21.
[2] John 12:47.

tradict their theological position. It is plainly obvious to most of the people listening to these endless debates that the Bible can't be validating two contradictory positions. There are only two options created by the current debates: either one view is correct and one is incorrect or both are incorrect and a third alternative must be sought. But for the last five hundred years or more both sides have been too stubborn to entertain the possibility that they may be wrong. So, the debate continues leaving the onlookers with the impression that it is legitimate to use part of the Bible, instead of all of it, to establish a valid view of any subject under debate.

It should be quite plain that those who hold to the universality of Christ's work on the cross have a much less difficult time explaining the passages that seem to limit the scope of the persons helped by Christ's death than the other way around. When the text says that Christ died for *all* nothing needs to be explained; the statement can be taken at face value. When the text says that Christ died for *some* or for *many*, but not for all, the universal or unlimited view only has to say that the *many* or the *some* are those out of the *all* who actually take advantage of the benefits that are provided for them by Christ's death.

On the other hand, those who hold the position that Christ did actually die only for *some* or only for *many* but not *all*, have a much tougher time explaining the universal scope of Christ's death. So, for example, they must use a cliché and repeat it very discriminately. That cliché affirms that Christ died for *all without distinction*, but He did not die for *all without exception*. But apart from the appearances that this cliché gives, those who use it understand that Christ did not die for all. The cliché is really misleading.

The outcome of the cliché's use is questionable. Isn't it basically saying that Jesus wasn't a racist, or a bigot, or a discriminator. He did not exclude any person or group of people from the benefits that His death on the cross provided. But, on the other hand, not all the persons within any particular group can be included as the beneficiaries of His death.

He died for all skin colors, but He didn't die for all of any one skin color. He died for all economic strata, but He didn't die for all within any one economic stratum. But neither Jesus' teachings nor His works ever call these things into question in the first place. This distinction, this discrimination, is certainly foisted upon the Scriptures rather than being a natural concern gleaned from them.

Generally speaking then, those passages which affirm that only some or many benefit from Christ's death describe the limited appropriation or reception of the available blessings provided by the death of Christ. While He died for all, each person must decide which aspects of Jesus' accomplishments he will believe in. And then he must trust the Holy Spirit to make these real in his own experience. There is always a difference between what God provides for us and what we actually experience in our lives. The presence of differing levels of maturity among the Christians that we know establishes that truth beyond a reasonable doubt.

But in the end, both sides are mistaken because they use the death of Christ to secure a heavenly destiny. And that is the one thing is certainly doesn't do. Not for all. Nor for some.

Chapter 7

Faith in Jesus Never Results in Forgiveness

In the third volume in this series, a chapter was given over to a discussion about the relationship of salvation to the forgiveness of a person's sins. The reader may need to review that chapter before going further. The following comments will be based upon that discussion.

Most will agree that Jesus' death was the fulfillment of certain aspects of the OT sacrificial system since the book of Hebrews describes it as the substance or reality of what the OT sacrifices foreshadowed.[1] And since there are obvious cases, many of them in fact, of people obtaining forgiveness without any mention of believing in a coming Messiah, forgiveness must not be dependent upon or related in any way to believing in the coming Messiah or in Jesus, the Messiah, after He had come.

Since the blood of bulls and goats can never take away sins,[2] in contrast to Jesus' sacrifice,[3] when forgiveness was occurring in the OT, it had to be based upon something else other than animal sacrifices. I am suggesting that *every time forgiveness was given by God and received by man in the OT that God was applying the results of the cross of His Son.* Jesus' death had been planned before the foundation of the world.[4] While it had not taken place yet in the history of man, God was dealing with people in light

---

[1] Cf., Heb. 8:1-5; 9:23-26; 10:1.
[2] Heb. 10:4, 11.
[3] Heb. 9:26; 10:12, 14, 18.
[4] 1Pet. 1:20; Rev. 13:8.

of what it would accomplish when it finally took place.[1] Some times God required *means to be fulfilled* when He gave it. At other times He did not.

This is a *revolutionary* thought although it is not new at all. I hope you are grasping its full significance. If my suggestion is true, then, whatever Jesus had accomplished by His death, God was applying to every single person who lived before the time of Christ and who was pursuing a relationship with God. This suggestion is consistent with the principle given to us in Rom. 3:25 which says,

> "… in the *forbearance* of God, He *passed over* the sins previously committed for *the demonstration of His righteousness* at the present time …" (emphases mine)

Our *forbearing* God was graciously forgiving the sins being committed from the foundation of the world.[2] *In passing over the sins previously committed*, God was forgiving them even though no sufficient payment for sins had been made. In His forbearance, God waited for His Son to make that payment for the sins that He had already been forgiving. When Christ died, the world could begin to grasp, as it contemplated the sufficiency of the death of Christ Jesus for the sins of all men, how God was righteous in forgiving sins before an adequate sacrifice had been given for them.

Both 1Pet. 1:18-20 and Rev. 13:8[3] tell us that Jesus, who was *foreknown* before the foundation of the world, was also reckoned by God to have been *slain* then as well. Why was He said to have

---

[1] Rom. 3:25.

[2] This forgiveness is conditioned of course upon man's pursuit of God, fulfilling whatever condition that God may have required to grant forgiveness..

[3] The Greek text is clear that "before the foundation of the world" should be attached to the nearest object which is "the Lamb who had been slain."

been slain before the foundation of the world? *To make possible God's application of the cross in forgiving sins (among other things) before the cross actually took place.* Together these three verses establish the truth that God used the cross, passing out its benefits to men around the world, before Jesus ever hung upon it. This truth argues for drastic changes to be made in doctrines that have been considered untouchable for over 1500 years. But because the world is shrinking and the nations of the world cannot escape one another, the time for this change couldn't be better.

Not only were people forgiven in the OT without believing in Jesus or in a coming Messiah, people were forgiven in the NT without believing in Jesus. In fact, Jesus taught His disciples to seek forgiveness from God the Father apart from any reference to Himself or to His coming work on the cross.[1] Read His words again very carefully and think about what Jesus is telling His own apostles to do.

> "Pray, then, in this way:
> *'Our Father who art in heaven, …*
> *'And forgive us our debts, as we also have forgiven our debtors.'"*

Jesus taught the apostles to seek forgiveness by asking the Father for it. He made no connection whatsoever between the forgiveness that they will need and His coming death that would provide the basis for the forgiveness. In other words, *forgiveness can be obtained by seeking communion with the Father with the intent of obeying His will.*[2] Jesus gave no condition requiring faith in Himself as the stipulation for obtaining forgiveness. Since Jesus is the one offering forgiveness in this way, it must be a valid means to obtain forgiveness. Furthermore, if it was valid during

---

[1] Matt. 6:9-15.

[2] After He taught them to pray, *Thy will be done*, He taught them to seek forgiveness.

His earthly ministry, can there be any objection raised to keep it from being valid before His day or after His time?

If the objection is raised that the apostles, who were being taught on prayer to seek forgiveness from the God the Father, had already believed in Jesus, and for that reason Jesus didn't have to require faith in Himself at this time, it is admitted that the objection is a half-truth. The apostles had already believed in Jesus. That is a fact. But that will not relieve, much less solve, the problem that is being raised here because, as we will see in a moment, their faith in Him did not include a belief in either His death or His resurrection. Their faith in Him was limited to their belief that He was their promised Messiah. That's all.

We also notice that Jesus forgave the paralytic's sins without inviting him to believe in Him as the Messiah, the Son of God.[1] Someone might object to my using the paralytic's forgiveness because, it might be argued, his sins could have been inappropriate responses to other people and have nothing to do with his relationship with God. That distinction doesn't seem to be Biblically legitimate for a couple of reasons. First, King David seems to tell us that all sins are between an individual and God even if they involve other people as well.[2]

Second, the long-standing distinction between temporal sins (and their consequences) and eternal sins (and their consequences) seems to be coming to an end. If justification is not what we have been taught, and if salvation is not what we have been taught,[3] and if there is no sentence of eternal condemnation placed upon any sin anywhere in the Bible, then every time forgiveness is broached in the Bible it is talking about the same

---

[1] Mk. 2:1-12.

[2] Ps. 51:4.

[3] Volume one and two dealt with justification and volume three dealt with salvation.

kind of forgiveness: *the need to have the barriers that sin builds between man and God broken down so that fellowship can be entered into once again.* This is the only kind of forgiveness that one can find in the Bible.

And in Mk. 11:25, like Matt. 6:14-15, forgiveness can be obtained from God by forgiving those who offend you. In neither of these instances is there any mention of believing in Jesus or in a coming Messiah in order to obtain the forgiveness in question. We are not led by the text of Scripture to believe that faith in Jesus is involved in any way in obtaining forgiveness of sins.

It is extremely enlightening to discover that *Jesus never once offered to forgive a person if that person would only believe in Him.* At no time in His whole earthly ministry can one find such a message as what we proclaim to the world as the gospel of Jesus Christ: *believe in Jesus and receive the forgiveness of all of your sins.* Often the message that is preached even goes so far as to promise that the sins that a person hasn't committed yet will also be forgiven the moment he first believes in Jesus. Again, Jesus made no such offers.

Nevertheless, it is true that Jesus did die *for sins;*[1] He died so that they could be *forgiven;*[2] and He died so that the Father would be *propitiated* for man's sins against Him.[3] But none of these passages require the idea that sins are forgiven only by faith in Jesus. The doctrine of propitiation is a formulation of the systematizing efforts of men as they try to understand and summarize the message of the Bible. Unfortunately, that *suspect tenet* is usually foremost in the gospel that we proclaim to all non-Christians. At this point it is obvious that we are trusting

---

[1] 1Cor. 15:3.

[2] John 1:29; Acts 13:38; Eph. 1:7.

[3] 1John 2:2; 4:10.

65

more in the conclusions of man's reasoning than in the *explicit* statements of God's Word because the Bible never actually says what we are preaching to others.

As I try not to repeat what I've said in the third volume, let me conclude with one general over all principle and a very telling example of it. What follows should be enough to convince anyone that the old forensic paradigm simply doesn't work and the conclusions that it has drawn about forgiveness and the death of Jesus cannot explain the actual historical situation set before us in the four Gospel accounts. The general principle is that *the obtainment (or experience) of forgiveness occurs repeatedly (solely?) without believing in the need for Jesus' death on the cross.* That is a strong statement, I know. But it is easily defended when the Scriptures are interpreted in their most natural and straightforward sense.

Surely that principle describes accurately the lives and ministries of the apostles that Jesus chose for Himself. The apostles did not want Jesus to die. In fact, when He predicted His coming death, Peter took Him aside and rebuked Him over that issue. But the situation goes further than that. Not only did the apostles not want Jesus to die, and that goes for Judas as well, they did not understand the reason that He had to die. This is easily defended from the Scriptures. Lk. 9:43-45 say,

> "But while everyone was marveling at all that He was doing, He said to His disciples, 'Let these words sink into your ears; for the Son of Man is going to be delivered into the hands of men.' But they **did not understand** this statement, and **it was concealed** from them so that they might not perceive it; and they were afraid to ask Him about this statement." (emphases mine)

Two forces are at work here: the apostles' own weak, distracted, and self-centered comprehensions and God's divine conceal-

ment (although it doesn't matter who the author of the concealment is).

Following this interaction upon Jesus' prediction of His own
death, comes another one in Lk. 18:31-34, which say,

> "And He took the twelve aside and said to them, 'behold, we are
> going up to Jerusalem, and all things which are written through
> the prophets about the Son of Man will be accomplished. For He
> will be delivered to the Gentiles, and will be mocked and mistreat-
> ed and spit upon, and after they have scourged Him, they will kill
> Him; and the third day He will rise again.' And *they understood
> none of these things*, and *this saying was hidden from them*, and
> they did not comprehend the things that were said." (emphases
> mine)

This is a very detailed prediction of Jesus' death. But the apostles were not needing more details to understand what Jesus
was saying to them. They were needing to break away from
their own perceptions and desires about the establishment of the
promised kingdom of Messiah and humbly receive by faith the
facts that He was revealing to them. This same concealment
shrouded all the city of Jerusalem who refused to receive Jesus'
basic message, His miracles, or His warnings.[1]

The apostles had believed in Jesus and had received eternal
life. Following the prevalent misunderstanding of Acts 16:31 (as
well as Eph. 2:8-9), we have called the apostles *saved* individuals.
There is, I suppose, no one who would believe that the apostles
hadn't received or experienced forgiveness by the end of Jesus'
ministry to them. Yet, none of them wanted Jesus to die, and
none of them understood why He had to die. Therefore, their
belief in Jesus did not include a belief in the necessity of His
death as the basis for the forgiveness of their sins.

---

[1] Lk. 19:41-42.

This portrayal of the apostles' lives set before us in the Gospels is transparently obvious. They had experienced forgiveness themselves. Jesus taught them how to pray to God for forgiveness, seeking it without reference to Him or to His coming death. They were given a pathway to forgiveness, one that Jesus Himself condoned, and yet, they did not have to believe in Jesus for that forgiveness to be received. They believed, based upon Jesus' teachings, that they could obtain forgiveness from God the Father if they simply prayed to Him for it.

Now we must ask the question "If the apostles obtained forgiveness apart from believing in Jesus for it, why couldn't others obtain it the same way?" It seems apparent that forgiveness is obtainable *because of* the death of Jesus; He died for the sins of the whole world. Yet, it also seems apparent that forgiveness is obtained *without trusting in Jesus* for it. In other words, Jesus provides for each person's forgiveness through His death, but no one has to obtain that forgiveness by believing in Him (or in the fact that He died so that his sins could be forgiven). God the Father grants forgiveness through various means, but the basis upon which the forgiveness can be offered at all is the death of His Son.

This means that those who have never heard of Jesus, much less believed in Him, can still be forgiven because Jesus' death can be applied to them by the Father. Jesus' death satisfies the Father[1] so that He can reconcile the world to Himself.[2] What is the means that they must fulfill in order to be forgiven? Whatever means that God communicates to them that He is requiring of them.

---

[1] 1John 2:2; 4:10.
[2] 2Cor. 5:18-21.

This is not a "one-means-fits-all" situation. If you have read volume three of this series, you have already learned that Christianity does not have a corner on the market for tickets to forgiveness or to heaven. The two exclusion passages of John 14:6 and Acts 4:12 have already been dealt with. It has been shown that neither passage can be used to require a faith in Jesus for forgiveness or for heaven. *By taking verses out of their contexts, we have created an exclusive Christian faith that God does not condone.*

While it is for certain that believing in Jesus is **never** the means to obtain forgiveness or to get a free pass to heaven, it is, nevertheless, the only means for obtaining eternal life. That is the reason God has commanded us to preach Jesus. The world is in desperate need of what He is offering.

If no one has to believe in Jesus to obtain forgiveness for his sins, then what is the message that you intend to share with the rest of the world when you share your faith? If all you know is the old forensic paradigm, you will find yourself with little to offer all those who need Jesus so desperately. Their need is not obtaining a free ticket to heaven through faith in Jesus. That ticket is offered by a fraudulent travel agency.

When you share your faith, are you telling people what Jesus has provided for them to handle their trials successfully? Are you telling people what Jesus has provided for them so that they can hear God's declaration, "Well, done, good and faithful servant!" That is the message that all people need to hear. That is the message the Bible presents.

Ultimately, your *evangelism* just got a lot tougher. You won't be able to pull off being the agent for the real Biblical message without some sacrifice. Are you ready to give that sacrifice? There will be no "hit and run" evangelism wrecking the future growth of the person who was supposedly saved. Evangelism, the kind the Bible charges followers of Jesus with, requires teaching all the things that Jesus taught His first disciples.[1] Our own faithfulness will make us adequate teachers[2] even though we will remain far from perfect.

[1] Matt. 28:19.
[2] 2Tim. 2:2; 2Cor. 3:5-6.

Chapter 8

God's Means for Obtaining Forgiveness

As the last chapter stated, God has required different means at different times for different people to receive the forgiveness of sins that He has provided through the cross of His Son. But not once did Jesus offer that same forgiveness if only a person would believe in Him. Nowhere in the earthly ministry of Jesus can a person find a challenge similar to "Believe in Me, and I'll forgive your sins." Yet we find Jesus forgiving sins *without* requiring people to believe in Him as Savior, or as Savior and Lord, or as the Christ, or in any other way.

He further taught His audiences that He had *authority* while He ministered on earth to forgive the sins that people commit. I, for one, have given too little thought on Jesus' point of having authority to forgive! This authority was His *before* He died on the cross. Does this authority extend backward into the OT? Does He share this authority, as His teaching on prayer suggests, with the Father? Authority to forgive! Before the cross! Authority to forgive! Without requiring faith in Himself!

Most of us have been taught that there are different kinds of forgiveness in the Scriptures. But one kind receives the most attention in our discussions. It is the forgiveness that *supposedly* removes the *eternal penalty* resulting from each and every sin we commit. This penalty is *supposed* to condemn the person upon whom it rests to an eternity in the fires of hell. This penalty is generally referred to as *eternal death*, and it is *supposed* to describe an eternal punishment[1] in a place of torment.[2] Such a position is fraught with unbiblical assumptions that will not stand the test of exegetical scrutiny any longer.

On the other hand, there is the kind of forgiveness that deals with our *daily estrangement* from God. This penalty describes a *temporal separation* (death) from God in which a loss of fellowship and a relinquishment of all the blessings that go with that intimacy transpire. This penalty is removed instantly when we confess our sins and begin walking in the light again.

Is the teaching on eternal punishment truly the best understanding of the Scriptures? Can you find a verse that *explicitly* says, "The consequence of each sin committed is an *eternal penalty, punishment,* or *place* of torment that will be obtained and endured"? And, on the other hand, can you find a verse that explicitly says, "The forgiveness that you obtain, however you might obtain it, frees you from *an eternal penalty, punishment* or *incarceration in* a *place of torment"*?

Or to put the matter more in theological terms we might say, "Are there two very different kinds of forgiveness described in the Scriptures, a *forensic forgiveness* that frees a person from an eternal punishment in hell, and a *familial forgiveness* that admits him back into fellowship with God while he lives his life upon earth?" Since we have shown in the previous three volumes that justification can no longer be portrayed as a once-for-all, courtroom declaration of *right standing* or *status before God,* there is no foundation for any forensic forgiveness as our orthodox Christian theology has formulated it to this point in history. Such a viewpoint is unsupported in the Scriptures. What we believe is

---

[1] Cf., Matt. 25:46.
[2] Cf., Lk. 16:23, 24, 28.

founded upon *presuppositions* and *assumptions* alone. The Bible will lead its reader in a very different direction if the errant presumptions are relinquished first.

The forgiveness that a person receives from God is *always* dealing with that person's relationship and walk with God. It never involves any kind of permanent standing or status before God. *To be forgiven is never a divine declaration of permanent guiltlessness.* If it were, then there would be no basis for God's judging each man's works after he dies. The fact that each man must stand before God in order to be judged, requires the conviction that what is forgiven is every obstacle that hinders a person's relationship with God as he lives his life now. Forgiveness has nothing to do with the afterlife; it does not give a person a "get-out-of-hell-free" card. But it is a "get-out-of-the-darkness-and-the-emptiness-and-the-loneliness-and-the-meaninglessness-and-the-purposelessness-of-life-free"card. And that card is not only reusable, it makes all of our lives worth living!

What are some of the means that God has ordained for men to obtain forgiveness from Him since He has not ordained faith in Jesus to accomplish that feat? Consider the following examples. You may have discovered more than these in your own study of the Scriptures.

Bringing the Proper Sacrifice

In the OT the primary method for obtaining forgiveness was by bringing the proper sacrifice to the priest for him to offer for the atonement of the worshipper's sins. The important point here is to notice that *after* the proper sacrifice had been offered to atone for the sins that have been committed, *then* God forgave the person bringing the offering. *The priest made atonement, but*

God forgave. Let's take a couple of verses from Leviticus to demonstrate the point here.

> "So the priest shall make atonement *for them* (the sins committed by the one bringing the sacrifice to the priest), and *they* shall be forgiven." (Lev. 4:20)

There does not seem to be a distinction being made between the sins committed and the sinner committing the sins. So, in Lev. 4:26 we see a parallel between the sinner and the sins he has committed:

> "Thus the priest shall make atonement *for him* in regard to his sin, and *he* shall be forgiven."

Consequently, it is appropriate to speak of both the sins being atoned for and the sinner being atoned for while the distinction is maintained between atonement and forgiveness: *the priest could atone for the sinner and his sins, but only God could forgive the sinner and his sins.* Notice that the priest is the subject of the atoning work while the forgiving work is put into the passive voice. Never is the priest the one doing the forgiving.

Repentance and/or Baptism

A second means of obtaining forgiveness was through repentance even if the repentance was manifested apart from any sacrifice required by the Mosaic Law[1] or water baptism.[2] So the fact that forgiveness can be found in the Scriptures attached to either the obedience of the Law or to water baptism should not be enough to divide the people of God.

When John the Baptist came upon the scene in the NT, the entire Jewish nation was still under the Mosaic Law. Yet, John

---

[1] Cf., Num. 14:19; Jonah 3-4.
[2] Cf., Lk. 24:47; Acts 3:19; 8:22.

preached a message offering forgiveness of sins through a different means than the sacrificial system of the Mosaic Law. Mark, recording Peter's recollections of the events surrounding Jesus' earthly ministry, explained it this way:

> "John the Baptist appeared in the wilderness preaching *a baptism of repentance for the forgiveness of sins*." (Mk. 1:4, my emphasis)

Now whether one wants to make the water baptism the means of forgiveness or the repentance the means, it seems to matter little since the two phenomena were so closely related that one is hard pressed to distinguish between the two. It is a fact that John required the baptism as an evidence of the unseen repentance. This was a forgiveness that was obtainable apart from the observance of the Mosaic Law. And that is the important point.

John's baptism was being offered to those who were already connected to the one true God, having been forgiven at least yearly at the Day of Atonement if not regularly as well through their sacrifices for their sins according to the Law of Moses. So, neither John the Baptist's message nor Jesus' message was for the *so-called eternally lost and condemned person who needed a deliverance from hell*. Rather, they both were sent to the people of God to draw them back into a spiritual walk that God could bless.

As the NT opened up, God's people were not persevering in their faith in a way that God could approve. For the most part, they were keeping the Laws that God had given them, but they were not mixing faith in their obedience.[1] This was the perpetual failure of the Jewish people as the Letter to the Hebrews so clearly tells us.[2] And we must not miss the fact that the author of this little sermon in the Book of Hebrews used it to warn believ-

---

[1] Cf., Rom. 9:30-33.
[2] Cf., Heb. 3:12-4:2.

ers in the church about this same tendency among them.

Prayer

Another means of obtaining forgiveness in both the OT and the NT was prayer. A person could simply pray to God and be forgiven of his sins. Listen to what Solomon prayed when he had finished building the new temple and was dedicating it to the God of Israel:

> " 'But will God indeed dwell on the earth? Behold, heaven and the highest heaven cannot contain Thee, how much less this house which I have built! Yet have regard to the prayer of Thy servant and to his supplication, O Lord my God, to listen to the cry and to the prayer which Thy servant prays before Thee today; that Thine eyes may be open toward this house night and day, toward the place of which Thou hast said, "My name shall be there,' to listen to the prayer which Thy servant shall pray toward this place. *And listen to the supplication of Thy servant and of Thy people Israel, when they pray toward this place; hear Thou in heaven Thy dwelling place; hear and forgive.'*" (1Kgs. 8:27-30)

Basically, this same prayer is repeated no less than four more times in this chapter alone: "Hear, God, and forgive!" Solomon clearly affirmed the principle that not all men (not even all Jews) would have the same requirements to fulfill in order to walk with God. In this case, some would not be able to come to the temple to offer a sacrifice for their sins. For them, prayer to God would be the means that they would use to obtain the forgiveness that they needed.[1]

Solomon gives seven examples to illustrate what he is asking God to do in the next twenty-three verses. Here is the second

---

[1] The same principle applies to the soteriological offer that Jesus gave re the kingdom.

example[1] that he gives:

> "'When Thy people Israel are defeated before any enemy because they have sinned against Thee, if they *turn* to Thee again and *confess* Thy name and *pray and make supplication* to Thee in this house (the Temple that Solomon had just built for God), *then hear* Thou in heaven, *and forgive* the sin of Thy people Israel, and bring them back to the land which Thou didn't give to their fathers.'" (1Kgs. 8:33-34)

Prayer was not to be taken as some guarantee of forgiveness any more than repentance or confession might be. But if these responses flow from a heart that has turned back to God and has become reliant upon Him once again, God will be successfully persuaded to hear, forgive, and deliver His people. *Solomon is asking God to forgive the sins of the Jewish people without having faith in a coming Messiah or of offering the sacrifices required by Law.*

Recall Jesus' teaching on prayer in the NT. His teaching on prayer in Matt. 6:9-13 is properly referred to as the Disciples' Prayer since it was given to the twelve apostles specifically to guide them in their prayer life. But Jesus expected them to pass on this model to everyone to whom they would minister in the future since *all men pray to the same God* even though they may have distorted His character and transformed His essence into perversions of the original truth that they had received from Him. King David wrote,

> "O Thou who dost hear prayer, *To Thee all men come.*" (Ps. 65:2)[2]

While all religions do not lead to God, they all have led away

---

[1] Note that the first one, 1Kgs. 8:22-32, clarifies the issue of justification in the OT: *God only justifies the one who is righteous already*. The orthodox Christian doctrine of justification, then, is unsupported. God justifies only the righteous who have faith in Him.

[2] This is the same truth that C.S. Lewis put into Aslan's mouth as he was confronting Emeth about his former service and prayers to Tash. *The Last Battle*, Collier Books, 1956, pp. 164-65.

from Him and the revelation He has given to each one of them. And for their distortions they are presently giving an account, and must one day be judged for exchanging the glory of the incorruptible God for the distortions they have imagined.[1] Consequently, they lose now, and they will lose further in the afterlife. But all religions, including Christianity, are susceptible to this same apostasy. Believing in Jesus will not prevent God's chastisement now nor will it avert God's judgment in the afterlife.

As long as a person acts consistently, extending forgiveness to each person who sought his forgiveness, he can expect God to forgive him when he prays for it.[2] A person does not have to be a Christian to follow Jesus' teaching on prayer. There is not one element of His instructions that cannot be followed by any person in the whole world. Because the Bible is very clear in both the OT and in the NT that *every person who fears God and does what is right is acceptable to Him,*[3] every person can come before God in prayer and know that He will be heard even on the matter of his own forgiveness. Both King Abimelech[4] and Cornelius[5] are the classic examples of this truth. King Solomon's comments in the Book of Ecclesiastes[6] *universalizes* this principle for every person around the globe regardless of his culture or religion. It is still true today *after* Jesus the Messiah has come and gone.

---

[1] Cf., Rom. 1:21-23.
[2] Matt. 6:14-15.
[3] Gen. 20:1-11; Eccl. 12:13-14; John 9:31; Acts 10:34-35.
[4] Gen. 20:1-11.
[5] Acts 10:34-35.
[6] Eccl. 12:13-14.

Touching Hot Coals to one's Lips[1]

This particular means of obtaining forgiveness may have been used only once in all of human history as far as we know. But the point is God could offer forgiveness this way, and it was just as effective as any of the other means that God chose to use. When Isaiah the prophet saw a vision of God high and lifted up, he cried out in distress of heart,

> "Woe is me, for I am ruined! Because I am a man of unclean lips, And I live among a people of unclean lips; For my eyes have seen the King, the Lord of hosts." (Isa. 6:5)

The following two verses explain God's response to Isaiah's overwhelming conviction of his sinfulness:

> "Then one of the seraphim flew to me, with a burning coal in his hand which he had taken from the altar with tongs. And he touched my mouth with it and said, 'Behold, *this has touched your lips; and your iniquity is taken away, and your sin is forgiven.'*" (Isa. 6:6-7, emphasis mine)

Admittedly, this is a strange means for obtaining forgiveness. But it is clearly set forth as one nonetheless. The question that naturally arises is this: "If forgiveness could be obtained by this means, as unusual as it is, what should we think of Christianity's teaching that the exclusive means of obtaining forgiveness is only through faith in Jesus?" Obviously, something is not correct here. Could our systematization of the teaching of the Bible be mistaken? Is it possible that forgiveness can be obtained in other ways? The answer seems to be all too clear, doesn't it?

---

[1] This author is aware that the Hebrew term used here is kaphar, rather than salach. It should be remembered, however, that while there is a major difference between atonement and forgiveness, each time an atonement was successfully made, forgiveness was also offered. Atonement was the requirement set upon man to fulfill in order to have God forgive him of his sins. The atonement never achieved forgiveness. God drew from the cross to forgive whenever an atonement was made that satisfied Him.

And we must not forget that this is the only kind of forgiveness that the Scriptures describe. The forensic paradigm has already been set aside as unbiblical in the previous three volumes. So, no objection can be raised here that this forgiveness is for the so-called *believer* rather than the so-called *unbeliever*. There is one forgiveness; it provides for divine fellowship.

Confession of Sin

It has long been a teaching of orthodox Christianity that forgiveness can be obtained through confession. 1John 1:9 clearly declares this to be so when it says,

> "If we **confess our sins**, He is faithful and just to *forgive our sins* and to cleanse us from all unrighteousness." (emphases mine)

Some, because of the previous teaching that they have received on this subject, may not see the point that I'm trying to make here. It does not matter that the text of 1John is talking about *believers* in Christ who were being instructed to seek forgiveness. All believers in God could obtain forgiveness the same way.

While all forgiveness is possible *because of* the death of Christ Jesus, and, therefore, all forgiveness is *through Him* (i.e., by means of His work on the cross), yet no forgiveness is obtained *by believing in Him*. That is the basic truth of Scripture. What Jesus did on the cross, He did for the whole world. Those who *believe in Him* are able to be forgiven just like those who *have never heard of Him*. By what He accomplished in His death on the cross, every man, who responds in faith to the revelation that God has given to him, can be forgiven. Out of His great, great mercy, God is applying the benefits of Christ's death to all who seek a relationship with Him.

Chapter 9

Photo-Clips of the Work of the Cross

According to most Christian theologies, the big terms, representing the major concepts about salvation, are all related and occur at the same moment in time. The thought is this: when a person initially places his faith in Jesus for salvation, at that moment justification takes place. And along with justification, redemption, propitiation (or expiation), and reconciliation take place also. In other words, while these are different matters and broach different aspects of "salvation," they all occur together at the same moment.

Let's assume for the sake of brevity that the simultaneous occurrence of all these things is true. What happens to these concepts if, as I have shown in the previous volumes, justification does not occur at *initial faith* in Jesus as it has been imagined? What happens to all these concepts if justification occurs not as a result of initial faith in Jesus or in God, but as a result of *continuing faith* in God or in Jesus? In other words, if justification cannot be demonstrated to occur at initial faith, then all the other concepts are also instantly changed from a single occurrence to repetitive experiences. That, don't you see, changes everything?

If justification is repetitive, then redemption, which is supposed to occur when justification occurs, is repetitive. If justification is repetitive, then reconciliation is repetitive if they occur together. If justification is repetitive, then propitiation (or expiation) is also repetitive. In short, if justification is repetitive, then all of these concepts relate to living a life of faith rather than coming to initial faith (whether in God or in Jesus).

The purpose of this chapter, then, is to help the reader to begin reevaluating how much of his soteriology (his understanding of the doctrine of salvation) is based upon the Bible and how much comes from the rational deductions that men have made in an attempt to tie their theology all together in a nice, neat package. There is nothing wrong with trying to tie the teachings of the Bible together in a nice, neat package, unless of course, some of the concepts don't really fit into the package and must be forced to fit like Cinderella's slipper. Like any other doctrine, there are some tenets that are clearly revealed and others that are reached only through a continuous series of deductions, conjectures, and suppositions based mostly upon extra-Biblical presuppositions. When we go beyond the Scriptures, we only deceive ourselves into thinking that we know more than we actually do and, eventually, create problems that become our own spiritual undoing, or the undoing of those who receive our teaching.

None of these issues can remain what they have been supposed to be, namely, *positional truths.* By that I mean that none of these issues are once-for-all, and none of them have to do with the believer's so-called *perpetual or eternal standing* or *status* before God. None of them have to do with God's judicial, once-for-all declaration of spiritual acceptance for all eternity.

While Christ's work on the cross is once-for-all, finished, complete, and unrepeatable, yet the application of its accomplishments to a person is repetitive. So, each time we stray from God, we need to be reconciled again. Each time we stray from God, we need to be redeemed again. Each time we stray from

God, we need Jesus to be our propitiation toward God and have His Mercy Seat extended toward us again. And, at least in a couple of senses, we need to be saved again. I'm not referring to being saved from hell, but from the power of indwelling sin and from the limitations of our own abilities, and possibly even from the entrapments of Satan himself.

If all this is true, then no one is in a *position* that is final. No one has a status or standing before God that does not need further applications of Christ's work on his behalf. No one has received a divine verdict that secures him from present divine chastisement or future divine judgment for his waywardness.

Every judgment described in the Scriptures is upon what a person has done during his lifetime. No judgment is upon what a person believes, or, to be more specific, whether he has believed in Jesus or not. That is just another disturbing fact of God's revelation to us. Consequently, *bad theology will not keep a person out of heaven*. Each person will still have to be judged for everything that he has done whether good or bad. He will also be judged for his bad theology as well as for his failure to carry out his good theology.

As we look at all the elements of the doctrine of salvation, we must realize that the Bible's presentation of these matters may be compared to looking at photos in a friend's family album. There are many things that are clear from each photo. But it is an obvious mistake to think that one knows everything that was happening by one photo when it was first taken. How each photo relates to every other photo must be determined by the person who took the pictures in the first place. No one who was absent when the photos were originally shot has the ability to explain how the photos connect with each other. And if the original photographer doesn't connect the storyline of the photos for us, it is best not to create layer after layer of conjecture about what *might* be true or what *could* have happened at the event being photographed.

Each of the concepts involved in the doctrine of salvation is a fairly disconnected, isolated picture of what is taking place. So, it will need an authoritative explanation if it is to be connected with precision to the other concepts. And if the original photographer has failed to give that explanation, as indeed He has at times, then great care must be taken not to read more into the concepts or into their connections with each other than has been *explicitly* given.

So, in a quite rapid and brief style, like photos being taken one right after the other, we will touch upon the major aspects of the doctrine of salvation. This is clearly an overview, reviewing basic elements that are related to the doctrine of salvation. And there will be no attempt to go beyond what is clearly stated in God's inspired Word to us. My deductions are no better than anyone else's.

Concerning Sin

One of the facts that every Christian knows is that Christ died *for our sins*. The classic passage declaring this truth is 1Cor. 15:3 which says,

> "For I delivered to you as of first importance what I also received, that Christ died *for our sins* according to the Scriptures . . ."

This tenet is not vague, nor is it complicated. Christ died *for our sins*. That is a fact that should not be debated, diluted, or rejected. But this classic passage does not give the *reason* that Christ died for our sins, nor is it explicit in describing *how* He died upon that cross. Did He die as our Savior, as our Substitute, or as our Sacrifice as He mediated our reconciliation to God? Or maybe He died as all three. If He did, the Scriptures must declare it plainly to us.

But the point that I want to emphasize here is this: we know that Jesus died *for our sins*. That is a fact of Scripture. But we are not told *in what way* (how) He accomplished what God the Father had sent Him to do on the cross. Nor are we told the *purpose* that He was accomplishing when He died.

Did He die to deliver those who believe in Him from an eternal penalty of condemnation or from a temporal penalty of spiritual separation?

Did He die so that the person who believes in Him can go to heaven?

Or did He die so that the person who believes in Him can rejoin God's family and walk in fellowship with Him as a heavenly Father who loves and cares for him?

Did He die for those who haven't believed in Him or even heard of Him?

This passage doesn't tell us any more than the fact that *He died for our sins*. It is only a snap-shot of one aspect of all that was going on at that moment. It needs the Original Photographer to clarify *in what way* and *for what reason* He died. If He doesn't, we must not photo-shop the picture!

Just because a reasonable answer can be given by someone presenting his particular view of Christ's death for our sins, it does not follow that he has given a Biblical answer. We must not be reasonably led astray! God's revelation alone must guide us. What we know is Christ died for our sins. Now we must look at another photo and have the Original Photographer connect the two photos for us.

A Propitiation of (or Expiation to) God for sin

Another fact of Scripture is that Jesus was sent by the Father to be a propitiation for man's sins and was publicly displayed by the Father as a Mercy Seat[1] through the offering of Himself upon the cross for our sins.[2] *He* ***is*** *the propitiation because of shedding His blood for our sins, but He* ***becomes*** *the mercy seat in real practice only for all who walk by faith.* This is the reason John says,

> "In this is love, not that we loved God, but that He loved us and sent His Son to be the propitiation for our sins," (1John 4:10)

and

> "And if anyone sins, we have an Advocate with the Father, Jesus Christ the righteous; and He Himself is the propitiation for our sins, and not for ours only, but also for those of the whole world." (1John 2:2)

But Paul added to this an additional thought:

> "… a mercy seat in His blood ***through faith*** …" (Rom. 3:25)

As the top of the ark of the covenant was in the OT, so Jesus became in His death: the place where (or the Person with whom) man could find mercy from God. In Christ, God stands ever ready to receive back into fellowship the person who responds in faith to Him. He is able to receive the sinner upon his return because Christ's blood has taken care of the obstacles that lay between them, namely, the person's sins.

In what way Jesus satisfies the Father, the Scriptures are silent so it is best not to connect dots that the Bible does not connect

---

[1] Rom. 3:25.
[2] 1John 4:10. Cf., 1John 2:2 as well.

for us. *It is enough to believe that Jesus is the believer's Mercy Seat and the satisfaction that the Father needed in order to offer Jesus as such.* Since God the Father sent Jesus to be a satisfaction for sins, and since Jesus came to fulfill the will of the God the Father, He must have done so in, apparently, a way that remains a mystery to us since it has not been revealed to us.

Since there is no passage that specifically connects the wrath of God to the death of Jesus on the cross for sins, there is no reason to prefer the term *propitiation* over the term *expiation*. Is God's wrath being poured out upon all unrighteousness and ungodliness of man today? Certainly.[1] But it does not necessarily follow that God must pour out His wrath upon Jesus who became man's sin bearer upon the cross. Since God is by nature a forgiving God,[2] He can act according to His nature (i.e., be forgiving) without being angry or wrathful in the process.[3] Whatever God needed to remove the obstacles created by man's sin and bridge the relationship from His side, He received through the death of Christ Jesus on the cross. These are the facts of Scripture. And nowhere is faith in Jesus required for receiving forgiveness.

A Redemption

When someone brings up the subject of redemption, most of us think of a deliverance from hell. And obviously if a person is delivered from hell, he must be going someplace else. Since there are *supposedly* only two ultimate destinations, it is *assumed* that a deliverance from hell also assures a person of a place in heaven immediately after he dies. Redemption in the minds of

---

[1] Rom 1:18.
[2] Ex. 34:7.
[3] Cf., Num. 14:11-25; 2Sam. 12:1-25.

many is no different from salvation or justification. All three of these terms are generally understood to refer to an escape from hell accompanied by a safe deliverance into heaven forever.

But if we allow the Scriptures to interpret the concept of redemption for us, as it clearly does in the story of the Exodus, then we have no reason to believe that redemption has anything to do with heaven or hell. Rather, redemption refers to God's deliverances which get us out of the messes we get ourselves into when we walk after our own desires for our own goals. *And depending upon the deliverance that is needed, God uses different means to extricate us from our particular bondages.* But all of those bondages relate to this life alone. Jesus' death on the cross freed mankind from indwelling sin now; it did not free anyone from judgment in the afterlife.

The redemption of Israel from Egyptian slavery was brought about by God's outstretched hand and His miracles. And even before Israel was freed, God promised to do this very thing when He said,

> "'Say, therefore, to the sons of Israel, 'I am the Lord, and I **will bring you out** from under the burdens of the Egyptians, and I **will deliver** you from their bondage. I **will also redeem** you with an outstretched arm and with great judgments." (Ex. 6:6)

It should be very obvious that this is not a description of any kind of *spiritual redemption*. This is a physical redemption from first to last. There is no mention of heaven or thought of hell or any need of the cross upon which Jesus died. When this deliverance ~ *this redemption* ~ was successfully accomplished, Moses wrote a song extolling God's *redemptive purchase* of Israel.[1] Moses' song was very appropriate since the redemption of Israel

---

[1] Ex. 15:13, 16.

from Egypt became the most important deliverance by God in Israel's history. All other deliverances would be compared to this one.

Everyone would love to know more about this physical redemption. But this is all that the snap-shot contains. And we must resist the temptation to photo-shop the snap-shot. We don't need to add anything to this picture; nor do we need to remove anything from it. God redeems in just this way! Israel, already designated as God's first-born son, will be released from their slavery by their God who has a unique plan for their existence. They have been ordained to serve Him as a depository and example of His revelation for a world that has lost its way. They will become the preachers of righteousness as Noah was before them.

One of the poignant passages on redemption is given to us by the apostle Peter. I will give the whole context to show that I am using it exactly how Peter meant it to be used. It says,

> "And if you address as Father the One who *impartially judges* according to each man's *work, conduct* yourselves in fear during the time of your stay *upon the earth*; knowing that *you were* not *redeemed* with perishable things like silver or gold *from your futile way of life* inherited from your forefathers, but *with precious blood*, as of a lamb unblemished and spotless, *the blood* *of Christ*. (1Pet. 1:17-19, emphases mine)

While the rest of 1Peter one and all of two focus upon exactly the same matter, namely, holy living, the verses quoted here establish that topic clearly. Many of the themes that I have been presenting are touched upon in this short passage. God is a Judge, but He will judge every person according to his own works, rather than according to his beliefs. Because that judgment is coming, all men ought to conduct themselves with fear just as Paul taught in 2Cor 5:10-11.

The second reason that Peter gives for living a holy life[1] is that every person has been redeemed by the precious blood of Christ. So, his thought is this: not only is God the Father going to judge us according to our works (and don't forget Peter is writing to believers who accepted the work of the cross on their behalf), He has already redeemed us by the precious blood of His Son "from our futile way of life." The redemption that God the Father provided through His Son was not from hell; it was *from the futile way of life*" that is lived apart from communion with a holy God. Just like Israel was redeemed from slavery, a futile way of life, so Christians today are in like manner redeemed from a futile way of life.

The point is simple: *redemption is from the various kinds of enslavements in which God's creatures entangle themselves.* Each person has been redeemed from whatever he had allowed to become his master. He may continue to serve that master when he is not pursuing communion with God. But he need not do so.

Interestingly enough, the apostle Paul describes the Corinthian Christians as those who have been bought with a price. But the important observation is the application he makes of that ransom price. The context for the following two verses focuses upon the lifestyle of the Christian. And specifically, it concerns sexual immorality. In that context, Paul said,

> "Or do you not know that your body is temple of the Holy Spirit who is in you, whom you have from God, and that **you are not your own?** For **you have been bought with a price;** therefore **glorify God in your body.**" (1Cor. 6:19-20, emphases mine)

---

[1] 1Pet. 1:13-16.

They were bought so that they might live holy lives, pure lives, free from sexual immorality. *Like the apostle Peter, the apostle to the Gentiles related redemption to being freed from immoral conduct.* Because they were redeemed from these kinds of sins,[1] they should now walk by the Spirit in all holiness.

A person doesn't see redemption as a heaven and hell issue when he reads the Bible unless he reads it into the context himself. Redemption is part of the work of God to free man from all the obstacles that could hinder his responsiveness to Him. There is no focus upon heaven or hell; the focus is entirely upon breaking down the barriers that hinder man's walk with God.

A Reconciliation

The discussion on reconciliation will probably be the least surprising. Most people understand what reconciliation means, and almost as many have had to walk through the process of reconciliation at some point during their lives. So, to suggest a radically different view of it would certainly seem strange to most. And the exciting point is our intuition about reconciliation is exactly what it means in the Bible.

If we use Col. 1:22 for our basic understanding of reconciliation, we can keep our discussion simple and uncluttered. First of all, we notice that the text relates reconciliation to the death of Jesus when it says,

> "... yet *He has now reconciled you in His fleshly body through death,* in order to present you before Him *holy and blameless and beyond reproach* ..."* (emphases mine)

But the key declaration here is found in the purpose clause that

---

[1] 1Cor. 6:9-11. It is also significant that Paul relates being washed, being sanctified, and being justified to matters of conduct.

Paul wrote. That purpose statement relates reconciliation to being *holy, blameless, and beyond reproach*. This passage does not connect the concept of reconciliation to anything related to the afterlife. It is related to living life a certain way. *To be reconciled to God is to live in harmony with Him and His will.* Paul does here exactly what he and Peter did with the concept of redemption: he related it to living life now rather than any concept related to being secure in the afterlife with an escape from hell and a guaranteed place in heaven. Reconciliation is about a return to God for the purpose of representing Him in all that we do as we have fellowship with Him. In short, it is about this life alone.

The concept of reconciliation was put in the past tense by Paul to emphasize a couple of facts. First, he and the Roman Christians had been reconciled to God at some point in their lives. Both the Christians in Rome and Paul had been brought back to God after they had, for whatever reason, left their intimacy with God to pursue a course in life that God could not justify. Second, having come back to God, they would not need to be reconciled again *until such a time arose when they had strayed away from Him again.* So, reconciliation is repetitive by the very fact that it deals with harmonic relationships.

Even the best of friends get cross-wise at times and need to be reconciled. The need arises every time someone has something against the other party, and that something is a big enough issue to come between the two parties and to sustain a break in their fellowship with each other.[1] If that sustained break produces alienation and hostility between the two parties, keeping them apart,[2] they will need to be reconciled again.

---

[1] Cf., Matt. 5:23-24.
[2] Cf., Col. 1:21-22.

Like the other truths, reconciliation, when it is dealt with theologically, has *assumptions* flowing from it that find little support in the Scriptures. So, for example, there is no indication that reconciliation is a one-time thing. There is no obvious proof that after it takes place, a situation cannot arise requiring it to reoccur. *And if the apostle Paul was urging the Christians at Corinth to be reconciled to God,*[1] *we have all the proof we need for viewing reconciliation as a potentially recurring phenomenon.* If they needed to be re-reconciled, and based upon the wickedness present within the church body there, it is obvious that they did, others likely have the same need as well. Reconciliation, like the other terms discussed in this chapter, is confined to a walk with God now.

---

[1] 2Cor. 5:18—6:3. The first person plural (*we*, along with the use of *our* and *us*) in verses 18-20, the purpose statement in v. 21 ("that *we* might become the righteousness of God in Him" and the clause in 6:1 ("*we* **also** *urge* **you**") demonstrate that Paul is challenging the Corinthians, and not some third party, to be reconciled to God. Because God's people can stray from God, they can need to be reconciled all over again. However, it is true that the whole world is in exactly the same situation as the Corinthians were in.

Chapter 10

The Victories through the Cross

It may be said, in general, that most of the important things to God are those things that He had His Son address when He died on the cross. The reason that statement is truth is that *in the cross God made it possible for man to fulfill the commission He gave him when he was first created*. After each man's sin, consequences occur that, if God did not take care of them immediately, man would not be able to fulfill that original commission: *to walk with Him and represent Him in all that he does.*

You might be shocked that the matter of heaven and hell is not addressed at all in this chapter because it is not addressed at all in the death of Jesus. Giving a person a free pass to heaven is not a matter on God's mind even though many people are obsessed with the question of their eternal destiny. God is concerned about the here and how. He is supplying everything that His children need to walk with Him spiritually. That is the reason for our existence. What is paramount on God's mind is a way to insure that such a walk can take place even after the Devil, sin, and death have entered into this world.

My goal is to set before the reader several major issues that Jesus' death on the cross dealt with in a sufficient and effective way even though it by no means dealt with these issues in a final way experientially speaking. Nothing else needs to be done to overcome these great enemies of spiritual life. But, as the next chapter will explain, walking in that victory is an entirely different matter altogether.

As a result, it is possible to have a victory that is not enjoyed.

It is possible to be delivered without experiencing the freedom that comes with that deliverance.

It is possible to be freed but still live in bondage.

That is the message of the Bible, and a reality that is ever before us as we struggle to live in the victory that we know that we already possess.

We will look at several issues in this chapter that the cross of Christ dealt with successfully. All other issues, I believe, can be subsumed under these. But more importantly, if these are properly understood, the daily life of each "believer" can be changed from victim to victor through the resources of Christ Jesus, God's unique Son.

It Dealt with Satan

There seems to be an unspoken anathema hovering over all who think that the cross dealt with Satan. The reason that it is inserted here at the beginning is that *it is the first issue that the Scriptures explicitly say that the coming Messiah will address.* God, who was walking with Adam and Eve in the Garden of Eden, prophesied that the Seed of woman, who most understand as a prophecy concerning the coming Messiah, would bruise (or crush) the head of the serpent while the serpent would bruise (or crush) the Seed's heel. Again, it is the common understanding that this bruising or crushing of the Messiah's heel refers to the cross. But that understanding is still nothing more than another assumption from the explicit message of this passage.

This view of this verse, like all other views, is conjecture to be sure. Since this crushing could be describing other aspects of the Messiah's ministry other than His cross, it is best not to rely upon this passage too much to indicate what happened at the cross. It is used here only because in the opening chapters of Genesis, God sets before us the four main objects or enemies that the Seed of the woman must conquer. And the first one is the Devil himself.

This victory over Satan might be a reference to Lk. 10:18-20 in Jesus' dialogue with the seventy disciples who were returning from their very successful, personal ministries:

> "And the seventy returned with joy, saying, 'Lord even the demons are subject to us in Your name.' And He said to them, 'I was *watching Satan fall from heaven like lightning*. Behold, I have given you *authority* to tread upon serpents and scorpions, and *over all the power of the enemy*, and nothing shall injure you. Nevertheless do not rejoice in this, that *the spirits are subject to you*, but rejoice that your names are recorded in heaven.'"

If this is the interpretation of Gen. 3:15, then the crushing of the Serpent's head is done through *the authority delegated by Jesus* to His faithful followers.[1] The last chapter in Paul's letter to the assemblies in Rome seems to expand upon this authority by suggesting that it is given to anyone who will walk in the power of the name of Jesus. This is a highly significant statement since the argument of Paul in Romans focuses upon how both the Jews and the Gentiles can walk righteously without being under the Mosaic Law. By walking righteously, the believer will keep Satan from hindering the future establishment of the promised Messianic Kingdom.[2] This kingdom will be the salvation, or physical deliverance, God has promised the whole world. Paul said it this way:

---

[1] Nevertheless, the effectiveness of this delegated authority could be based upon what happened at the cross. More of this line of thinking in a moment.
[2] Cf., Mk. 4:13-15; Lk. 4:5-8.

"Now I urge you, brethren, keep your eye on those who cause dissensions and hindrances contrary to the teaching which you learned, and turn away from them. For such men are slaves, not of our Lord Christ but of their own appetites; and by their smooth and flattering speech they deceive the hearts of the unsuspecting. For the report of your obedience has reached to all; therefore I am rejoicing over you, but I want you to be wise in what is good, and innocent in what is evil. And *the God of peace will soon crush Satan under your feet*. The grace of our Lord Jesus be with you." (Rom. 16:17-20)

The persons that Paul was warning the Romans to keep their eye on were those who wanted to continue fighting over the place of the Mosaic Law in the life of the believer, especially as it related to the amoral issues of life. This was the problem that Paul was seeking to solve when he wrote this letter; this was the problem that gave rise to the question of the place of the Mosaic Law in the life of the church age believer. Could a righteous lifestyle be attained without submitting to the Mosaic Law? That was the question that occasioned Paul's thorough address to the Roman assemblies.

The believers at Rome can crush Satan under their feet if they live by faith, applying the principles that Paul gave them to govern their view of Christian liberty and their participation in the grace that was available to them. Satan doesn't have to win any of the spiritual battles he brings upon believers. He can be crushed each and every time he mounts an offensive. *But it is by faith that the victory is won experientially by the believer.*

It is also possible that the prophecy of Gen. 3:15 is fulfilled in Jesus' return to earth. At that time, Satan is bound and thrown into an abyss for one thousand years.[1] Or the prophecy could be fulfilled after the initial binding of Satan for a thousand years

---

[1] Rev. 20:1-15.

when Satan is released to tempt God's people once again. After that offensive is overturned, Satan is thrown into the Lake of Fire. This could be a description of the ultimate crushing of Satan.

But the reality is that none of these Scriptural events are clearly related to the prophecy of Gen. 3:15. Nevertheless, the important point here is the fact that the crushing of Satan has to do with this life alone. The cross, as we will see in a moment, is the means that God used to subjugate Satan and all of his angelic followers. Authority over him (and them) is delegated to God's servants as they live righteously by faith.

When we look at the titles that the Scriptures give to the Devil, we should be impressed. Paul calls him "the prince of the power of the air."[1] He seems to be the first rebel against God, taking with him one third of all the other angels God created.[2] Under his leadership then are the other spiritual rulers, powers, world forces, even all of the spiritual beings of wickedness in the heavenly places.[3]

The apostle John refers to the Devil as the evil one[4] and declares that "the whole world lies in his power."[5] Even though the phrase "in the power of" is not in the original Greek text, it seems to grasp the issue accurately since John has formerly called the Devil "the ruler of this world."[6] Unfortunately, the Bible doesn't explain how the Devil is, or in what way he became, the ruler of this world. But that it seems to be a fact is seen from the Devil's third temptation of Jesus. Matthew gives the

---

[1] Eph. 2:2.
[2] Rev. 12:3, 4, 9.
[3] Eph. 6:12, 16.
[4] 1John 2:13, 14.
[5] 1John 5:19.
[6] John 12:31.

account in these words:

> "Again, the devil took Him to a very high mountain, and showed Him *all the kingdoms of the world,* and their glory; and he said to Him, 'All these things *I will give You,* if You fall down and worship me.'" (Matt. 4:8-9, emphases mine)

How did all the kingdoms upon the earth become the Devil's to give to whomever he pleased? In what way were they his? What kind of rulership did he exert over them? Were they his possessions, or were they more like his vassals? The Scriptures simply don't give us those answers. But we tend to fill in the answers by our best *conjectures* and then teach those *assumptions* as truth.

Apparently, at the cross Jesus *disarmed* and *triumphed* over the Devil and his angels.[1] Even so, their activities were not culminated at that time. Their activities will continue until the end of human history.[2] The verdict concerning them has been given so that even they know their judgment is coming.[3] But the complete execution of that verdict is still on hold. It would be, as it has been, a great mistake to underestimate the power of a defeated foe.

By triumphing over all the spiritual beings that have opposed God since their first sin and resultant fall, the cross freed all men from Satan's enslaving purposes. But each man must, nevertheless, decide for himself whom he will serve each day.[4] One can be delivered from the kingdom of darkness[5] and voluntarily return to it to live a life in darkness,[6] in the sphere in

---

[1] Col. 2:10, 15.
[2] 1Cor. 15:24.
[3] Matt. 8:29.
[4] Cf., Joshua 24:14-15; 1Kgs. 18:20-40.
[5] Col. 1:13-14.
[6] John 3:19-21.

which Satan rules.[1]

It Dealt with Indwelling Sin

It should seem fairly clear that God meant the cross of Jesus to deal with the change in man's constitution that resulted from his first sin. In two passages we are told that Jesus died to take care of something called *sin*. And this sin is different from the individual sins that a person commits. Although this entity is traditionally called man's *fallen, sinful nature* or just his *sin nature*, since that term is not used in the Bible, it is best that we use only those terms that the Bible used to identify it.[2]

We can speak of *sin* or more specifically of *indwelling sin*, but we should not speak of a sin nature within man. In fact, *the Bible never says that man's nature has become sinful*. But it does refer to *something inside of man* that is *never identified as his entire nature per se*, and that something has, indeed, become utterly sinful.

Rom. 6:8-10 tell us that Jesus died with reference to this thing called *sin*. Paul's exact words are these:

> "Now if we have died with Christ, we believe that we shall also live with Him, knowing that Christ, having been raised from the dead is never to die again, death no longer is master over Him. For the death that He died, **He died to sin**, one for all; but the life that he lives, He lives to God." (emphasis mine)

Expositions of Romans chapter six have led more people to personal, spiritual victory than any other passage in the Bible. For nearly one hundred and twenty-five years, there have been conferences held around the world focusing on Romans six through eight especially. And in my own ministry of more than forty-five

---

[1] 1John 2:7-11, 13, 14.

[2] I thank my spiritual mother, Sandy Edmonson, for teaching me this truth even before I understood its significance.

years, it has been my experience that when people understand their freedom in Christ from the indwelling master called *sin,* their lives are radically transformed. So, it is my hope that the current series of theological discussions will bring us full circle back to the Bible's emphasis upon living spiritually. It is this kind of living that God is concerned about as the greater volume of the Scriptures attest to constantly.

When Jesus died, Paul tells us that He *"died to sin."* If we simply stay in the context of Paul's letter to the Roman Christians, we will see that the *sin* that Paul is talking about is not an act of sin or a habit of sinning in a certain way; *he is talking about something inside of each person called (indwelling) sin which has the capability of ruling over a person's body, including all of its members* (mind, emotions, will, conscience, and these represent all that a person does, all that he feels, all that he thinks, and the value judgments that he makes).

Jesus died to sin even though He did not have sin Himself. *He had what sin is before it becomes sinful at the moment an individual first sins.* Jesus' death, His physical death, overcame sin once and for all.[1] Rather than descending into the abyss of theological conjecture about what sin is exactly and how it relates to the rest of man's constitution, there are facts that we can know even though myriad curiosities are left without answers. Physical death overcomes *this part of man's human nature* by taking it to the grave to remain while man's spirit and soul ascend into the presence of the Lord without its presence or influences.

How does Jesus' physical death to sin help us though? Only physical death makes indwelling sin's mastery within inopera-

---

[1] That implies that physical death, rather than being part of the negative consequences of sin, is a blessing from God since through it man is delivered from indwelling sin.

tive. To put all men in the position of having an alternative to its mastery, God united them spiritually to the death of Jesus. By doing this, God could *reckon* or *account* them as having died to sin through their union to Jesus' death to sin. *No one has to obey (indwelling) sin because its necessary rulership has been set aside through the physical death that God has reckoned upon him.*

When Jesus came up out of the tomb, His humanity had a new body and a wholly new nature, neither of which was "of this world." Both were immortal and imperishable, made for the world after death. His body and that part of His human nature called indwelling sin in sinful man were *left in the grave.*

The sin that indwells us remains in us as long as we are physically alive. But we can reckon ourselves to be dead to it because of our union to Christ's death. When He died, we died with Him. We can live today similarly to how we will be able to live after we actually die.

Jesus' death freed us from the tyranny of indwelling sin even though it remains with us as *a part* of our constitution. It is not the whole of our immaterial constitution; it is only *a part* of it. That is the reason the Bible never identifies indwelling sin as our whole *human nature.*

The Bible is very clear that our death with Christ Jesus was for the purpose of setting aside *the body of sin* so that we might no longer serve this thing called (*indwelling*) *sin* which remains within us until we physically die ourselves.[1] To the extent that we live lives that are dead to sin and alive to God is the extent that we will live righteous lives. All men have the power to live righteously because Jesus' death on the cross conquered this thing called *sin.*

---

[1] Rom. 6:6.

What are the sinful habits that characterize the responses that you give to the situations that arise in your life? Anger? Inferiority? Pride? Arrogance? Jealousy? Lying? Distrust? Lovelessness? A failure to forgive? Bitterness? Fear? Resentment? Impatience? Anxiety? A lack of self-control? Whatever your sin pattern is the good news is this: by your union to Christ's physical death, God has freed you from that part of your nature that produces those sinful responses. You can live today the way that you will live when you finally stand before God: without sin, without regret, without shame, but with all the love that you have always desired to express but have come so short of it.

It Dealt with Personal Sins

You can see that the way I've already dealt with indwelling sin also deals with our personal sins. Having dealt with indwelling sin through the physical death of Jesus on the cross, God has freed us from all the personal sins that naturally flow from indwelling sin's rulership within. Our personal sins flow out of us when we've set aside our intimate fellowship with God in order to follow the suggestions of indwelling sin within. The opposite of experiencing a close communion or fellowship with God is the experience of spiritual death. When Adam and Eve ate of the forbidden fruit, they died spiritually, and they died instantly. It is this death alone that fulfilled the warning that God had given to Adam and Eve.

There is no mention of heaven or hell in any of God's interactions with mankind's first parents. There was *no debt or penalty* with which they needed to concern themselves beyond the instantaneous death that had separated them from the fellowship that they had been experiencing with the God who had personally walked with them in the Garden. There was *no eternal penalty or debt incurred* in the first sin or in any subsequent sin by Adam and Eve or by anyone else who has ever lived. *The only debt that anyone incurs when he sins is the same spiritual death that came upon Adam and Eve when they sinned.*

While God is by nature a forgiving God, yet sin is a stain or defilement that requires it to be cleansed away[1] so that the sinner can move back into the presence of God to intimately commune with Him as he performs consecrated service for Him. God has already done everything in the death of His Son that was needed so that man could return to fellowship and to service. Why has He done all this? Because He is by nature a forgiving God and longs for the fellowship of His creatures, all of whom He calls His sons when they are fulfilling the revelation that He has given to them.

Jesus' death takes away (or removes or forgives) the sins that create a barrier between man and God. And this benefit of His cross is applied to every man who returns to God to walk with Him once again. If there is a condition for the application of Christ's death to him, God has made that plain to him. So, if he fulfills that obedience, when there is one, his sins are forgiven and his fellowship with God is renewed. Of course, God can also apply the death of Christ without the sinner fulfilling any condition at all as He apparently did in the case of Adam and Eve.

It Dealt with Spiritual Death (Separation from God)

It is difficult to actually talk about indwelling sin, personal sins, and spiritual death separately because they are so closely intertwined. Indwelling sin is the source for the other two: per-

---

[1] 1John 1:7.

sonal sins and spiritual death. If indwelling sin can be avoided, that is, if it can be set aside and not followed or relied upon, then personal sins will cease and spiritual death will no longer occur, must less be characteristic of the well-meaning Christian.

Indwelling sin is the source or agent of all of our sinful activities, dispositions, and states. Because it is *a part* of our human constitution, we are responsible for whatever we do by it. It can take something that is holy, righteous, and good, like the Mosaic Law, and misuse it so that spiritual death and personal sins result.

In the same way that it can misuse the Law of God, it can take our minds, our emotions, our wills, and our consciences, and use them to fall short of God's desired will for our lives. As a result, our thoughts are less than what God wants us to think; our emotions are less than what God wants us to feel; and our wills, following our errant thinking and our destructive feelings, respond in ways that don't bring glory to God. *Nevertheless, in all aspects the members themselves ~ our minds, our emotions, and our wills ~ do not become sinful themselves through this misuse any more than the Law does.*

Only indwelling sin is sinful, but it is extremely so.[1] Consequently, the Spirit of God can take the same mind, the same emotions, and the same will and produce through them a righteous life that is pleasing to God.[2] The Christian does not have two minds to think with, or two sets of emotions to express feelings with, or two wills to respond by. He has one mind that certainly at all times needs to be renewed, one set of emotions from which the corrupting responses need to be given up and healthy

---

[1] Rom. 7:13.
[2] Rom. 6:12-13.

emotions implanted in their place, and one will through which all actions take place. If the Spirit of God is infusing the life of Jesus with His thoughts, with His emotions, and with His enabling power into our wills, our responses will be what God's own Son would give if He were standing in our place as we act. The issue is not simply WWJD (What Would Jesus Do?); the issue is WIJDTURN (What Is Jesus Doing Through Us Right Now?).

When a person follows the enticements and desires of indwelling sin, whether in thought, feelings, or willful response, neither his thoughts, his emotions, nor his willful responses will be what God desired them to be. His responses will be sinful because indwelling sin has taken his members captive and has produced unrighteous responses through them.[1]

And as soon as indwelling sin takes the throne of a person's life as his king,[2] even before an outward sinful action is performed or an inward emotion is felt, the person has died;[3] he has become separated from God and from all of His resources. He finds himself in this dilemma: he still needs to respond to his present circumstances in a way that would please the God while he has separated himself from God and from His resources.

This spiritual separation is what the Bible refers to as spiritual death. It is not related to man's capability; it is related to man's communion with God and his reliance upon Him (or the lack of these experiences in his life). It is a temporary reality experienced by all men, including those most devoted to God. *Because all men (even those who have believed in Jesus) experience this phenomenon called spiritual death, it can't have anything to do with*

---

[1] See Rom. 7:23 and Rom. 6:16, respectively.
[2] Rom. 6:12-13.
[3] Rom. 6:16, 23.

107

man's capabilities. It rather describes whether man's capabilities are being exercised in communion with God, relying on Him to supply to his soul all that is needed to experience spiritual victory, or whether his capabilities are being exercised separately from Him.

It is unfortunate that there are no alarms or sirens that go off when this is taking place. But then, if there were, the noise would probably make worship on Sunday impossible for all the rest as well.

Chapter 11

The Victories Won may not be Experienced

On May 8, 1945 news was broadcast that the German high command had met with Allied officials and had signed surrender papers the previous morning. This surrender was made known to the troops on the ground in the months that followed. And a formal surrender of all the German civil governments followed as well. Yet it was another three months before the Japanese officially surrendered on August 15, 1945 after two atomic bombs were dropped on their country. Western Europe and the United States celebrated as never before.

The end of the war clearly designated the winners and the losers. When peace was declared, the two hostile factions were to put down their weapons and cease fighting. Since the non-aggressors had won, they were ready to move on. The aggressors were glad that the consequences of the war had not been more severe for them. So, they too were glad to lay down their arms. Well, most of them were.

But there was a group of four soldiers who had only months before been sent out into the field with a special assignment.[1] When they were commissioned, they were forbidden to surrender or to take their own lives. Regardless of how hard the battle became, they were to continue fighting until their commanders,

_____

[1] This story was retrieved at
file:///Users/daletaliaferro/Documents/Japanese%20Soldier%20Who%20Continued%20Fighting%20WWII%2029%20Years%20After%20the%20Japanese%20Surrendered,%20Because%20He%20D.webarchive on March 16, 2015.

who had commissioned them, came back for them. At the time of their commissioning on December 26, 1944, the Japanese were certain that they would win the war.

The commander of the insertion force was Hiroo Onoda, a twenty-year-old draftee. The group was sent to the island of Lubang in the Philippines. When they were inserted onto the island, they linked up with other Japanese soldiers already there. On February 28, 1945, just two months after his insertion, Allied forces landed on the island and shortly thereafter conquered all the Japanese forces except three or four small groups which retreated into the jungle to escape. Onoda led one group.

In October of 1945 over two months after Japan had surrendered, Onoda found a leaflet from the local islanders saying,

"The war ended August 15th. Come down from the mountains!"

The surviving soldiers discussed the leaflet but decided that it was Allied propaganda, trying to deceive them so that they would give themselves up. Japan couldn't have lost the war so quickly after their deployment to the island, they concluded.

The locals were getting tired of the guerrilla warfare instigated by these remaining Japanese soldiers so they were able to get a Boeing B-17 to drop leaflets all over the jungle, containing a command from General Yamashita to surrender. This was followed by further drops of more leaflets, newspapers from Japan, photographs and letters from the soldiers' families. Then delegates from Japan came to the island. These hiked through the jungles, speaking on loudspeakers, begging the soldiers to surrender.

After five years one of Onoda's cell of four soldiers surrendered without telling the others. Onoda and the others thought he had been captured. Now there must be, they thought, a security threat so they retreated further into the jungle.

Five years later another of Onoda's cell was shot and killed on the beach. This was proof to the others that the fighting was still going on. But now only Onoda and Kozuka were left.

For the next seventeen years the two lived in the jungle and continued gathering intelligence for Japan. One day Kozuka was killed in a fight with a Filipino patrol. This occurred sometime in October of 1972, twenty-seven years after the war had ended.

After the Japanese sent a search party to find Onoda and were unsuccessful, in 1974 a college student by the name of Nario Suzuki decided to travel the world. One of things on his to-do list on his travels was to find Onoda. Amazingly, where others had failed, he succeeded. He found Onoda. But he would not surrender or come out of the jungle until his commanding officers came to the island as they said they would and commanded him to come out.

During the 29 years of his insertion onto the island and his guerrilla warfare, he had killed thirty Filipinos, injured over one hundred others and destroyed various crops. So, when his commanding officer Major Taniguchi, who now worked at a book store, came to the island and convinced him to lay down his gun, he would still need to be pardoned for all the crimes he had committed during those 29 years by the Philippine President Ferdinand Marcos. And on March 10, 1975 Onoda, dressed in full uniform, came out of the jungle and surrendered his samurai sword to President Marcos.

In fighting after the war had been lost, Onoda represents man's four great enemies: the Devil, indwelling sin, spiritual death, and personal sins. Like Onoda, these have killed, injured, and destroyed. Also like Onoda, they have all been defeated already. Even their continuing assaults can be successfully repulsed if one is consistent in his walk of faith in the Lord.

The believer's four enemies have all been defeated at the cross of Jesus. But they are also still fighting a battle that they can't possibly win. In fact, they are fighting a battle that they have already lost! Nevertheless, they can do enormous damage and create a lot of heartache before they lay down their arms forever.

The Devil has been defeated, but he is continuing to wage war against anyone who wants to serve God. Indwelling sin has been defeated, but it continues to lure and entice the believer each time a task of obedience is undertaken. Spiritual death and all of our personal sins can be avoided even though they remain the natural results of indwelling sin's engagement and rule within man's soul.

While Onoda was a defeated foe, he still actively worked to defeat those who opposed him. We know that these foes exist because the Bible discloses this information to us. We know how they are defeated in the same way we know they exist. Now we must believe these truths and act according to them as we face these enemies whenever they rise up to fight against us.

While the cross is the means that God used to defeat all of our enemies, nevertheless, more is involved for the believer to *experience* the victory that the cross has won for him. Think of it like this: the two bullies, the Devil and indwelling sin, that have made our lives miserable for as long as we can remember, are secretly approached by God Himself. He tells them that their unrestricted right to bully us has ended; He tells them that He has freed every man from their power and authority so that no one has to obey them any longer.

But instead of forbidding them to have any contact with us at all, He allows them to have as much access to us as we are able to bear *if* we are walking in dependence upon Him. So, they are no longer able to *force* us to do anything that is contrary to the will of God for our lives. But their *intimidations* are very . . . well, intimidating, and their *enticements* are very seductive. Consequently, we can and still do yield to them all too often.

Because we were not present when God met with them and limited their authority over us, we have to take it by faith that He actually did this. Often their overtures to us are so strong that we are uncertain by the looks of the situation and by our own feelings that we have really been freed from them and don't have to succumb to their intimidations. But that mind-set and those emotions are the result of walking by sight rather than walking by faith. How different our lives would be if we kept the mind-set that the bullies that look so mean really have no authority over us any longer.

Because of God's meeting with the bullies and His restricting their authority over us, they cannot make us do anything. They can only lead, entice, lure, or intimidate us to follow them. But they can't make us follow them. We must agree on our own to their overtures. When we do, we follow them when we didn't have to. We obey them even though they have no authority over us. We listen to them even though they have no right to demand anything from us. God's meeting with them solved the problem on one level, but our choice to either believe and obey God or believe and obey them addresses the problem on another level, the practical level where life is actually lived out. Without a walk of faith we will still live in bondage even though God has already taken care of the problem. If we don't walk in light of what God has already done for us, we will try to do what we are incapable of doing, defeating our enemies. And our experience will be that of Rom. 7:15-25.

Battling the Devil, our External Defeated Foe

When we look at the titles given to Satan in the Scriptures, we naturally wonder what they can mean. If he is the *ruler* of the world,[1] for example, does that mean he has some authority at some point over all men born into the world? When did this authority first commence? What does it include? How can it be terminated?

When we read that the whole world lies *in the power* of the evil one, we wonder what is the extent of his power over any particular person, don't we? When Paul says that the battle today is not against flesh and blood but against the spiritual forces in the heavenly places,[2] we wonder how can a human win a battle over super-human forces?

While most, if not all, of these questions are unanswerable, what we know for certain is that Jesus' death overcomes every obstacle to a personal reconciliation with God.[3] So *if* there was a bondage to Satan that resulted from man's first sin (or from any subsequent sin), the cross frees him from Satan's bondage. *If* Satan had become each sinner's master as a consequence of his first sin, that mastery was broken by the death of Christ Jesus on the cross. *Whatever authority or hold* Satan may have had over the sinner due to his first sin, it has been set aside and has ceased forever as a necessary consequence. Why? The cross triumphs

---

[1] John 12:31. Also see supra, pp. 101-102.

[2] Eph. 6:10-12.

[3] 2Cor. 5:18-19; Rom. 5:10-11.

over all the principalities, powers, and wicked forces in the heavenly places.[1] *If* Satan's rulership over the whole world included direct command over each person who sinned, Jesus' cross nullified that necessary rulership by the redemption that was accomplished in His death.[2]

Maybe there was no rulership or mastery by Satan over man in the first place. That is certainly possible. But when we interact with the concepts of *"world* rulership" and *"everything* lying in the power of the evil one," it is certainly natural to ask, "How far did Satan's power and rulership extend?"

We are not required, on the other hand, to conclude that Jesus paid a ransom to Satan for our release (redemption) any more than God paid a ransom to the Egyptians to redeem Israel from slavery. While the ransom may describe *what it cost God* to free us today and what it cost God to free Israel thirty-five hundred years ago, it may be more accurate to say that the ransom was *laid upon* Satan for us today as it was *laid upon* Egypt in the past rather than that it *was given to* Satan today or Egypt earlier. So just as Egypt did not gain anything by the redemption that God made to purchase Israel from slavery but rather was despoiled by Israel in the process, in the same way Satan did not gain a ransom payment for the release of men from his spiritual captivity, but rather suffered a great loss in the whole affair.

Though the Devil was defeated at the cross, he may still come after those whom he has lost rulership over, just like the Egyptians did after God redeemed Israel from Egyptian slavery. The Egyptians came after the Israelites to capture them at the Red Sea and re-enslave them. So, the apostle Peter warns all the

---

[1] Col. 2:15.
[2] Rom. 3:24.

dispersed Jews, the audience to whom he was writing, to stay alert in the spiritual battle that is raging on every hand because the enemy is coming after you to re-enslave you:

"Your adversary, the Devil, prowls around like *a roaring lion,* seeking someone to devour." (1Pet. 5:8, emphasis mine)

But not all of the Devil's approaches are as overt as a roaring lion coming after its prey. The apostle Paul warns the Ephesians that they must . . .

". . . stand firm against *the schemes* of the Devil." (Eph. 6:11, emphasis mine)

One element of those schemes, Paul tells the believers in Corinth, is to approach men deceptively, even using deceitful workers in the ministry. Paul explains,

"For such men are false apostles, deceitful workers, disguising themselves as apostles of Christ. No wonder, for even *Satan disguises himself as an angel of light.* Therefore it is not surprising if his servants also disguise themselves as servants of righteousness, whose end will be according to their deeds." (2Cor. 11:13-15, my emphasis)

And the gist of all this scheming and maneuvering couldn't be better illustrated than in the first two chapters of the Book of Job.

Why talk about what could have been but what never came about? Why discuss a bondage to Satan as the result of sin if it never really came about? The answer is that it demonstrates how great the love of God is for every single human born into the world. He created all men to have fellowship with Him as they pursued their course in life, representing God in all that they did. So, to make sure that a relationship with God can still happen even after they sin was the design of the cross; it took care of the problems that arose after sin had come into their lives so that they could hear from God and respond to Him all their lives. If someone doesn't take advantage of that relationship with God, that person alone is culpable because God has provided a way of escape.[1]

Battling Sin, our Internally Defeated Foe

Not only have the spiritual beings in the heavenly places been defeated at the cross, indwelling sin has been also. But it is one of the Church's biggest mistakes to believe that sin is no longer a problem to be overcome on a daily basis. *The apostle Paul spent the first eight chapters of his letter to the Romans explaining that indwelling sin is the primary cause of unrighteous living.* For both the Gentile, who did not have the Law of God, and the Jew, who was given the Law through Moses, indwelling sin was the real cause of their unrighteous living. The issue was not whether either group had the Law or not.

If the cause of unrighteous living is indwelling sin, then the problem that the Jews had during the time of Jesus was not their intent to obey God, but their failure to succeed in doing what they actually wanted to do.[2] Likewise, the Gentiles at the time of Christ had an intent to respond to God in worship, as Paul's experience at Mars Hill shows us,[3] but their indwelling sin caused a great deal of failure in their worship. The Gospel of John, 4:23-24, helps us here by explaining that God has always sought men who would worship Him in spirit and truth (rather than by indwelling sin, following the lies it invents as Cain did in the worship he offered in Gen. 4:1-8). Their shortcomings in worship

---

[1] 1Cor. 10:13.
[2] Rom. 10:2-3.
[3] Acts 17:22-31.

represented the rulership of indwelling sin over their hearts, not the intent of their hearts.

A solution to indwelling sin had to be put in place, or man would not have been able to fulfill God's original commission to him: *commune with Me in intimate fellowship while you live your lives on a daily basis, representing Me in all that you do.*[1] Man's redemption deals with Satan and (indwelling) sin. Both have been conquered so that man can walk with God and represent Him in all that he does.

Even though Jesus conquered indwelling sin at the cross, nevertheless, just like the Devil, it is still present to entice and lure,[2] to deceive and distort.[3] While its necessary power over man has been broken,[4] just like Satan's, it can still rule over him by the various means just mentioned. Overcoming indwelling sin is the key that opens the door to an abundant, spiritual life. Such a life can be lived two ways today: by walking by faith in God rather than by walking by faith in indwelling sin, or by setting indwelling sin aside[5] on a moment by moment basis[6] by having the Spirit of God lead, empower, and grant virtues[7] that extend beyond anything that man can produce on his own. This life must be learned and then diligently implemented.

---

[1] Volume one showed that God's approach to Cain is based upon the cross' applicability.
[2] Js. 1:14-15.
[3] Rom. 7:7-25; Heb. 3:12-14.
[4] Rom. 6:8-10, 18-20, 22; 8:3.
[5] Rom. 6:6.
[6] Gal. 5:16.
[7] Gal. 5:16-26; Rom. 8:4-6.

Chapter 12

Substitutionary Atonement, a Theological Idea

It had never occurred to me until a couple of years ago that my belief in a substitutionary death by Jesus Christ was almost wholly a theological, rather than an exegetical, conclusion. Sure I was taught about certain eminent exegetes who did theses on this topic, but the scope of these papers, as I gave them more thought, are not as convincing as I was first led to believe. Really the evidence merely demonstrated what could possibly be true.

The exegetical evidence for the substitutionary death of Christ is not so persuasive that the student walks away saying, "This is the only reasonable position to hold." In fact, all of the exegetical evidence combined adds so little support to the horse's hair holding the sword of Damocles that its fall should have been long ago expected.

For centuries the substitutionary death of Christ has been the most precious and powerful doctrine within the Christian faith. Its continuance, however, actually hangs by the smallest thread because it lacks the *explicit*, exegetical foundation that makes it truly unassailable. To base such an important doctrine upon two prepositions and what they *could* mean is entirely insufficient for anyone who is not already committed to the doctrine. To read the OT sacrifices, even those offered on the Day of Atonement, as though they required a vicarious or substitutionary meaning, is gratuitous at best. And finally, to use the passages that say mankind's sins were laid upon Christ upon the cross *as man's substitute* is to seek support from the very passages that lead the student of Scripture in the opposite direction.[1]

There is no one who presently believes this doctrine, I believe, who couldn't take the opposing view, playing the Devil's advocate, and win the argument. So why is this doctrine seen to be so essential to Christianity? The reason is entirely, or almost so, theological: the present-day understanding of the message of the Bible as *a forensic paradigm* in which God the righteous (and wrathful?) Judge is deciding the eternal destiny of all men based upon whether they have believed in Jesus as their substitute, who took upon Himself the punishment that was due to them. This paradigm desperately needs a substitutionary death to make it work.[2] But apart from that paradigm, there is no other theory of the death of Jesus that needs to make Jesus' death a vicarious or substitutionary event.[3] This is a case in which the end (*a guarantee of heaven*, which many call *eternal salvation* as Ryrie does) justifies the means (a Substitute taking all of God's punishment so that the one who believes in this Substitute can be free of punishment and gain an escape from hell and with it the free gift of heaven).

But what do we do if the forensic paradigm is not even val-

---

[1] L. Berkhof, *Systematic Theology*. Wm. B. Eerdmans Publishing Co., Grand Rapids, Michigan, 1941, fourth revised and enlarged edition, pp.376-78. These are the standard points made for a defense of Christ's cross as a vicarious or substitutionary death.

[2] Charles Ryrie, *Basic Theology*, pp. 308-9. "While there may be truth in views that do not include penal substitution, it is important to remember that such truth, if there be some, cannot *save eternally*. Only the substitutionary death of Christ can provide that which God's justice demands and thereby become *the basis for the gift of eternal life* to those who believe." All this is moot if there is no "eternal salvation" as Christian theology demands. It is to be understood that Ryrie holds to the substitutionary death theory.

[3] Both Gustaf Aulen in *Christus Victor*, pp. 84-92, and Mark Baker and Joel Green in *Recovering the Scandal of the Cross*, IVP Academic, second edition, pp. 151-61, make the argument that Anselm's view of the atonement (as satisfaction) is not the same idea of substitution as is found in the penal, substitutionary view (as satisfaction).

id? That is what we want to test in this chapter. Is the assumption of a forensic paradigm, into which all the details of the Bible have been forced, a valid idea?

If God isn't judging men based upon whether they have believed in Jesus, then the forensic template, that has been set on top of the Bible in order to understand it, has actually led us astray.

If God isn't declaring men's destiny with one rap of His gavel, then the forensic paradigm is inadequate to explain the message of the Bible.

If justification is not really a part of that judicial, once-for-all declaration, then the forensic paradigm has no exegetical basis at all.

If there is no *necessary* inclusion of forgiveness in the act of justification, then the forensic template loses its basis for giving an eternal pardon to man.

If salvation is not even about obtaining from the divine Judge a place in heaven, then the forensic mold for understanding the Bible is incapable to explaining God's message to His creatures.

If God's plan all along was to have all men die with Christ on the cross, then there has to be special pleading to make Jesus' death a substitutionary death.

And finally, *if* there is no penalty, resting upon any sin, which extends into the afterlife and for which Christ needed to die, the forensic paradigm is misleading at best.

What does the Bible actually say about the death of Christ Jesus our Lord? And we must understand that *what it never says about the cross shouldn't be a part of our belief system.*

No Evidence of a Spiritual Courtroom

I'd like to begin by looking at the big picture and then move down to the details. So, as we read our Bibles, the question that I'd like to ask is this, "Have we come across a forensic passage that shouted out to us that God was judging the person, that we were reading about, like a judge in a courtroom, and in doing so was determining that person's eternal destiny?" That is what the forensic paradigm says that the Bible does. But I have found no passage that, without the aid of my reading into the context some theological grid, presented such a situation to me. Not one.

Is this the picture that you got when you read about Adam and Eve? Or Cain and Seth? Or Noah? Or Abraham? Or Isaac? Or Jacob? Or David? When was the first time you came upon a man, or a group of men, or even a whole city or nation, standing before God the great Judge of the whole world receiving his (or their) verdict from God concerning his (or their) eternal destiny? Remember what we're after here: *if the whole Bible is to be understood from a forensic paradigm, then the whole Bible ought to be filled with pictures of that paradigm.* But that is not really what we find in the Bible, is it?

When we get to the NT, we are faced with another problem. And it is a quite significant one. While there are lots of reasons for why Jesus came to earth, one thing He did not come to do was judge anyone with respect to the afterlife even though all judgment had been given into His hands. Listen to what John said about Jesus' coming to earth relative to judgment:

> "For God did not send the Son into the world to *judge the world*, but that *the world should be saved* through Him. He who *believes* in Him *is not judged*, he who *does not believe* [or is not believing] *has been judged already*, because he *has not believed* in the name

of the unique Son of God." (John 3:17-18, author's translation and emphases)

We should notice that the judgment that is taking place has to do with this life, not the afterlife. That is the great focus of the Scriptures. Walk in the light now. If you walk in the darkness, you will miss out on real life and the blessings of God that accompany real life. You will also be required, as all of God's creatures will be, to enter into judgment after you die. And that judgment will be about how you lived your life, not about whom you might have believed in (Jesus) before you died.

When Jesus does talk about a final judgment, He describes it as a judgment upon each man's deeds rather than upon the content of his faith. Jesus described this future judgment this way:

> "Do not marvel at this; for an hour *is coming* in which all who are in the tombs shall hear His voice, and shall come forth; those who did the *good deeds* to a resurrection of life, those who committed the *evil deeds* to a resurrection of judgment." (John 5:28-29)

The judgment of John 3:17-21 is carried out during a person's life on this earth. Every decision that is not of faith is condemned by God.[1] But the judgment of John 5:28-29 is still in the future. It is the judgment upon all those who had already died, and it centers wholly upon the deeds that they had done while they had been alive.

The temporal consequences arising from the sins we commit do not seem to be identical to the consequences that come upon us at the Judgment Seat of Christ after we die. The temporal consequences of the sins that we commit while living on earth can be *graciously dismissed* altogether by God, if He so desires, so that we might even feel like we have gotten away with the sin

---

[1] Rom. 14:23. Cf., Heb. 11:2, 6.

that we had committed.[1] The consequences pronounced upon us at the Judgment Seat of Christ are based in God's *justice* so that every sin is given its own *recompense*.[2] No sin is overlooked; no sin gets a pass from God. The coming of such a judgment is a sobering thought indeed!

There is no forensic courtroom anywhere in the Scriptures, portraying a Judge who promises heavenly destinies to those who believe in Jesus (or in a coming Messiah), and who warns of hell for all those who don't. All of the final judgments described in the Bible are based upon the works that a person has done; they are not declarations of *acquittals* or *pardons* or of a *righteous standing* before God that is given freely *apart from works*.

These two passages are only illustrations of the point I'm making here. *A forensic paradigm* is the result of layer after layer of *assumptions*, some of which will be addressed below, added to a *hypothesis* that is *presumed* to adequately explain the Scriptures. The big picture is simply this: the *courtroom background* that is *presumed* to explain the message of the Bible can't be found by the average student of the Bible. It just isn't there to be found.

Justifying the Wicked or Guilty is Forbidden

Now to the big picture we can add a general principle that directly contradicts the premise upon which the forensic paradigm is based. Let's look at Deut. 25:1-2 and Prov. 17:15.

"If there is a dispute between men and they go to court, and the judges decide their case, and they *justify the righteous*[3] and *condemn the wicked,* then it shall be if the wicked man deserves to be beaten, the judge shall then make him lie down and be beaten in

---

[1] Cf., e.g., Isa. 40:27; Ps. 73:1-9.
[2] 2Cor. 5:10.
[3] Cf., also 1Kgs. 8:32.

this presence with the number of stripes according to his wickedness." (Deut. 25:1-2, with its marginal reading)

"He who *justifies the wicked*, and he who *condemns the righteous*,
both of them alike are an abomination to the Lord." (Prov. 17:15)

When a courtroom scene is presented to the reader of Scripture,
it is clear that the person who is justified is the person who is
already in the right (that is, he is already righteous), and the person who is condemned is the person who is in the wrong (or
wicked). God does not condone justifying the unrighteous or
condemning the righteous. But this is exactly what is taught in
the penal, substitutionary theory of Christ's death.

In the forensic paradigm, the wicked, ungodly person is
brought before God. If that person has believed in Jesus, then
God justifies the wicked, ungodly person because of what Jesus
did for him on the cross. What is *assumed* to take place just before God the righteous Judge raps His gavel and decides the
eternal innocence or eternal guilt of the person before Him two
enormous changes in the person standing before Him. 1.) God
forgives all of this man's sins (and removes all the penalties that
were due because of those sins) and 2.) He gives this person
Christ's very own perfect righteousness to "clothe" himself with
in the place of his own sinfulness. Consequently, Christ's righteousness is seen and judged rather than the guilt and sinfulness
of this man's own life.

When God finally gives His verdict upon this person, He
sees standing before Him *an already forgiven person* who stands in
the *perfect righteousness* of Jesus. Then, *supposedly*, according to
God's own righteousness, He justifies or declares that person
righteous who has no righteousness of his own. In addition,
since he is forgiven at this very moment so that he has no sins
nor any penalty resting upon his for his sins, he is thought to be

guiltless. What is being declared righteous is what has come to him through the faith that he placed in Jesus.

The traditional, orthodox position of historic Christianity is that justification includes a forgiveness of sins and an imputation of righteousness from Christ to the believer so that God can justify him and be righteous Himself in doing so. But notice that *at the heart of this theology is the admission that God only justifies the righteous just as Deut. 25 and Prov. 17 declare.* God forbids any other principle being used. There is not one instance in all of the Scriptures in which the term justification is used of a wicked person getting an approval by God.

Yet Christian theology is asking everyone to believe that in this one case it is the correct thing to do. We are asked to believe that *the theological formulation of men* is able to present an exception to the *explicit* statement of an inviolable principle of Scripture and of God's character. Those who hold to this Christian doctrine certainly don't see it this way, of course. So, the issue becomes this: do the details of this theological formulation represent the teachings of the Scriptures or will they, like the formulation itself, seem to contradict the clear statements of God's Word?

The general principle, like the big picture, states in no uncertain terms: *God does not justify the ungodly.* Period. So, if the details that we will discuss below prove to be inadequate to support any exception to the general principle, we must return to the beginning and admit that Reformed, Christian doctrine has contradicted the clear revelation of God's Word.

Justification is not a Forensic Issue

Now when we look at some of the terms that are supposed to convey this courtroom scene, we don't actually find them used in a forensic way at all. In my opinion, the whole forensic paradigm rests upon an unbiblical understanding of the term justification (and the verbs to justify and to reckon). *Supposedly, justification pictures that courtroom scene in which God forgives a person's sins and imputes to him the perfect righteousness of Jesus Christ.* That these *suppositions* are pure *conjectures* is quite easy to discern. My previous three volumes have argued against the traditional understanding of justification as a courtroom phenomenon so I will make this relatively short.

Abraham's justification is the first one given in the Scriptures,[1] and it is, according to the apostle Paul, to be used for all justifications for all times.[2] *No justification will ever be different from the one Abraham experienced.* If you are not familiar with it, you should turn to Gen. 15:1-6 and study it carefully. The apostle Paul, when he wrote to the Christians in the Roman assemblies, spent a whole chapter explaining Abraham's justification and what it entailed. And, if the last half of chapter three of Romans is taken into account, we have a chapter and a half of inspired explanation concerning justification. But rather than being too technical, I would have you look back at Gen. 15:1-6 as you ask yourself several questions:

Can you discern any courtroom scene here?

Is Abraham standing before God as his eternal Judge?

Has God pointed out any sins of Abraham?

Has God indicated in any way that those sins have been forgiven?

What, specifically, is reckoned to Abraham?

What was it reckoned as or for?

---

[1] Gen. 15:6.
[2] Rom. 4:22-25.

Is there any mention of Abraham's need to be righteous *before* the reckoning was made?

Doesn't this episode in Abraham's life look like a typical interaction between a person pursuing God and God who is commending that pursuit?

The most important observation of all may be the fact that this is *not Abraham's initial faith in God*. He had been following God ever since he was called to leave his home in Ur and go to the land of Canaan. So, it had to be sometime in Ur that Abraham had begun to develop his relationship with God. And if we think about how God works today, would we not expect that Abraham had begun to consistently believed in God for some time before he was called to follow God and move to another place to serve Him? Does God call the so-called *unbeliever* for service? Does God call the person who is not growing in his relationship with Him to be instrumental in the out working of His plan? Not usually. Not typically. Why *assume* then that God is doing this with Abraham? Why *assume* that God is calling a person who has just placed his faith in God for the first time and is an infant, spiritually speaking?

But the orthodox, Christian position on justification is that justification occurs at initial faith in God when all of that person's sins are forgiven and a perfect righteousness is given to him because he has none of his own. But this is not what was happening to Abraham in Gen. 15:6. This was not his *initial* faith; this was an example of his *continuing* faith. It is completely gratuitous to understand this event as describing Abraham's initial faith in God. There simply is no evidence for that view anywhere in the passage.

And if you read the passage carefully, you will notice that

Abraham was being justified because he had responded properly to God. In simple terms, God had given Abraham a promise of a multitudinous progeny, and Abraham believed that God would do what He promised to do. That is what Abraham's justification involved. And that is the whole of it. Furthermore, according to the apostle Paul, there is no other kind of justification before (or by) God. Our justification must be like Abraham's.

So where does that take us? It takes us back to *the suggestion* that by believing in Jesus, God can somehow justify the ungodly and not violate His own character and the principle according to which He works. *That suggestion has to be false* because justification does not involve what Christian orthodoxy says it does. Since justification does not include the forgiveness of sins and the gift of a perfect righteousness, it cannot sidestep the inviolable principle that God does not justify the ungodly.

No Evidence of an *Eternal* Debt

The forensic paradigm *assumes* that upon each sin that a man commits, God lays a penalty of eternal condemnation. So, the smallest sin imaginable merits an eternity in hell just like the deeds of the most wicked person one can imagine. *Every sin is given the same eternal punishment in the forensic paradigm.*

Have you really come across a declaration anywhere in the Bible that hell is merited as the result of one sin? Do you see the courtroom of God handing out verdicts of hell because of either a sin committed or because of a rejection of Jesus? It is important to be specific here. Closeness doesn't count. In the courtroom scene that you find in the Scriptures, *assuming* that you find one, is God explicitly condemning a person to hell for all eternity because of one sin or even because of a lifetime of sinning?

I have not found enough *hints*, much less direct statements, in the Scriptures to warrant a pursuit of such a study. As I focused on this issue more fully, I was surprised at what I found. *The only penalty for sin that I can find in the Scriptures is spiritual death.* By that I mean a spiritual separation from God and His resources *in this life* so that life must be handled without His aid or blessing. The only spiritual death I find is the one Adam and Eve experienced in the Garden of Eden. I don't ever find an additional penalty to that one. I don't find a sentence to hell thrust upon the person who has sinned regardless of how much they have sinned. The Bible is about this earthly life; it is not about the afterlife.

There is an afterlife. People will go to heaven, and others will go to hell. But neither destiny is the result of believing in or rejecting Jesus Christ as God's Messiah, Son (or any other title you want to add to this list).

Since Christ's death does not deal with the consequences that will be incurred in the afterlife, the forensic paradigm has no more attractiveness to it than any other theory of Christ's death. Some of those who have received eternal life by believing in Jesus will still go to hell. Some of those who have never trusted in Jesus will go to heaven immediately after death and begin their service to God. Jesus' death simply doesn't relate to or solve those issues at all.

God Intended All Men to Die with Christ

The next thought, that questions the validity of the forensic paradigm, that I want to set before you is the fact that *God always intended all men to die **with** Christ.* That was His plan before the foundation of the world. He never intended for Christ to die *in* *the place of* mankind. He always intended that Christ should die *for the benefit of* all men and that all men should *die with Him.*

That benefit, for the purposes that we have for this study, includes two major blessings. First Christ died to defeat that part of the human constitution that resides in all men, namely, indwelling sin. From Adam and Eve through all the descendants that come from them, God's intention was to have them all die with Christ so that after their first sin, *if* they should sin (and they all did[1]), they would not be in spiritual bondage to the change that took place within their constitutions.

This part of their human constitution called indwelling sin would have naturally and necessarily ruled over them if Christ had not conquered it through His death on the cross. Now, because God united all men to Christ in His death, indwelling sin must await permission to be given to it by man's soul to take charge over it. Whenever this happens, indwelling sin rules over the whole man and produces both spiritual death and personal sins, keeping the person from experiencing God's blessings.

Christ died for all men's sins. His death would provide the basis for God to forgive the sins and receive them back into fellowship. But because they all had died with Christ, they were freed from the necessary tyranny of indwelling sin and were able to return to God as they followed God's conviction and drawing. So, rather than having Christ die in man's place (so that man would not have to die), God had all men die with Christ so that they could pursue the revelation that He would continue to give them for returning to a life-changing fellowship with Him. This was God's intent for all men from the beginning. He made sure by the cross that it would not be overturned.

---

[1] Cf., 1John 1:10.

The Forensic Paradigm and the Historical Situations

One of the biggest obstacles that the forensic paradigm has to overcome is the historical context of the first century. Jesus is first and foremost the Jewish Messiah. He came to those who were already trusting God to send a *Redeemer* in the same way that He had sent Moses to the Israelites to *purchase* them out of Egypt with a strong right arm and mighty miracles.[1] In short, then, their *freedom* (or *redemption*) came from the power of their God to deliver them. Our freedom comes the same way today; God's power is seen both in the cross for spiritual deliverance and in His miraculous deeds for physical deliverance.

But if we use the forensic paradigm consistently, we have to conclude that Jesus came to those who would have already been justified and redeemed by God as well as reconciled to Him because they had already believed in the coming Messiah-Savior-Redeemer. Do not the Scriptures *explicitly* tell us that the Jewish people that He came to were already God's people?[2] Even the Samaritan women that Jesus encountered at Jacob's well believed in the coming Messiah.[3] And are not the chief priests and scribes included in God's people as well since they too believed in the coming Messiah and even knew where He would be born?[4] Nevertheless did not many, if not most, of *these same people* reject Jesus as the apostle John so clearly tells us that they did when he said,

> "He came to His own [things], and *those who were His own did not receive Him.*" (John 1:11, emphasis mine)

---

[1] Ex. 6:6; 15:13, 16.
[2] Matt. 1:21; John 1:11-12.
[3] John 4:25, 29, 39-42.
[4] Matt. 2:4-6.

If the forensic paradigm were true, then the first century Jew who had believed in a coming Messiah would have been justified *before* Jesus ever came upon the scene. So, when that same Jew rejected the Messiah when He came and presented Himself, what would have happened to his justification? If justification is an eternal, unchangeable status or standing before God, how could that have changed even if Jesus was rejected? Would not that future sin have been covered in his justification?

The historical situation of the Jewish people in the first century simply won't fit into the forensic paradigm. This historical problem is, at least currently, unsolvable with the present formulation of the forensic paradigm.

The Universality of the Cross Creates a Problem

I have already demonstrated from Scripture earlier that Jesus came to die for the whole world. But that universality does not fit well with the forensic paradigm. Consequently, to believe that Jesus' death was a substitutionary death many interpreters have to create a way around the universality of the cross. One way of sidestepping this universality, as I mentioned before, is the use of an appealing cliché: *Christ died for all without distinction, but not for all without exception.*

When John the Baptist identified Jesus as "the Lamb of God who is taking away the sin of the world," he means exactly that: the death of this Lamb (Jesus) would enable God to take away the sin of the whole world. When the apostle John said that God so loved the world that He gave His Son over to death that "whoever believes in Him should not perish but have eternal life," he distinguished between two very important, but very different, things. Jesus was given by the Father for the whole world in a way that the whole world could benefit from His death. But the one who believes in Jesus has yet another benefit that he can claim: eternal life. While the whole world has an interest in the death of Christ for the forgiveness of sins and for the defeat of Satan and indwelling sin, yet only those who have believed in Jesus can experience eternal life.

Christ died for all without exception. That is the clear message of the Bible. So, if Jesus died for all, and if, as the forensic paradigm tells us, His death had to be a vicarious death, dying in the place of another and bearing the penalty for everyone for whom He died, then the whole world must receive the benefit of the cross. *The forensic paradigm should lead to a universalism if the universality of the cross laid down in the Scriptures is accepted at face value.* But with or without the forensic paradigm, we have found throughout this series that God has made universal application of the cross even before Jesus died upon it. Because He has, our message to the world must change a bit. Much more of this topic is in the fourth volume of this series.

Chapter 13

The Facts Call for a Change

Hopefully these four volumes have been sufficient to cause you to reconsider the message of the Bible and the proper template that will best unfold that message. I was never aware of the number of *assumptions* that my belief system was based upon until I began restudying the Bible with the Missouri State slogan as my guide: *just show me!* What we have been taught was well-meant, but it has created a major barrier between Christianity and the rest of the world. We do not have the corner of the market for truth as the forensic paradigm has led us to believe. We need to begin separating what has been *assumed* to be truth from what the Bible actually says is true. And, if you are like me, that is not an easy road to travel. My former training has erected a wall between me and God's truth on several key issues, and it is an exhausting struggle to climb over that wall. But I am so glad to find more and more people already climbing that wall. They are all encouragements to me.

I would like to list for you most of the truths that I have been covering in this series. I have tried to present a fresh and relentless pursuit for the truth. These truths are not listed in any precise order even though I generally follow the linear graphs given in volume two of this series. It will be quite obvious that if these principles are acknowledged as true, a considerable change will have to occur in our own theological thinking. May this series and the following list help start that dialogue anew.

There is no point at which anyone in the Bible expresses initial faith in God.

This means that no one is ever presented as moving from an *unbelieving state* to a *believing state* relative to God Himself. As a result, it is impossible to know what happens at *initial faith* since no occasion of it is ever presented to us in the Bible for us to study.

There is no verse that says that when a person believes in God or in Jesus, he obtains a place in heaven as a free gift.

Isn't it interesting that Jesus never invited a person to believe in Him in order to obtain a place in heaven? Jesus didn't come to do that. He came to invite people back into fellowship with the God of heaven.

There is no verse that says that when a person believes in God or in Jesus that he escapes an eternity in hell.

Jesus never invited a person to believe in Him in order to obtain forgiveness of sins so that he could escape going to hell. Even though that is usually the first thing that a Christian tells a non-Christian ~ *believe in Jesus so your sins can be forgiven* ~ neither Jesus nor His disciples ever gave such an offer to anyone. Jesus did warn people about the consequences of unbelief and sin but those consequences were all temporal. Admittedly, some confusion does set in at this point since Jesus does warn about Gehenna and hell. But that warning is not related to one sin, but rather to a lifetime disposition of either indifference to God or rebellion toward Him.

There are significant examples of believers not persevering in their faith.

Most of the nation of Israel at different times and for whole generations did not persevere in their faith. But as I have shown in volume one of this series, God declared that Israel remained through all of those times His people. Even for the most ardent supporter of the doctrine of the perseverance of the saints, King Solomon remains an impossible obstacle to his belief. See God's testimony of his spiritual apostasy in 1Kings chapter eleven. Drawing prodigal sons back into fellowship is actually what the Bible is all about.

There is no obvious courtroom background to Abraham's justification.

Justification is *supposed* to be a courtroom scene in which the great Judge of the whole earth declares the eternal innocence of a person, not because he is indeed innocent, but because he has trusted in Jesus Christ who *supposedly* took the penalty of his sins and bore it on the cross. In doing this He paid all that was demanded by the Judge for all the sins the man had committed. By believing in Jesus, the sinful man could come before the Judge with payment in hand, so to speak, and be forgiven and declared righteous (in right standing).

But in Abraham's justification, he was not convicted of any sin, nor did he receive Another person's righteousness as his own. Rather, it was *Abraham's faith* that was reckoned to Abraham *as righteousness*. Nothing is involved in this first justification recorded in the Scriptures but what Abraham brought to the table himself. God reckoned or accounted Abraham's response of faith for righteousness.

There is only one kind of justification in the Scriptures that may occur one of two ways.

The apostle Paul made it clear that everyone is justified in exactly the same way that Abraham was. Since his justification was a declaration upon his response to God, so will ours be. Sometimes there may be no work or deed that is done as in Abraham's response to God's promise of a great progeny. But usually there is a work that is done as in Abraham's response of offering up Isaac upon an altar. But in either case, justification is God's declaration that *the response given was acceptable to Him*, one that He actually evaluates as righteous since it was given in faith.

Based upon Abraham's justification model, there is no imputation of Christ's righteousness to the person who believes in God or in Jesus.

Abraham's faith was "imputed" or reckoned or accounted for righteousness. There is no mention of a righteousness being given to Abraham. Rather the verse clearly says that *Abraham's faith is all Abraham needed to be reckoned by God as righteous.*

Based upon Abraham's justification model, typically there is no forgiveness of sins involved in justification.

Not only is there no courtroom scene or sense to the passage on Abraham's justification, there is no forgiveness involved at all. And this is the model for all justifications for every age. The forensic paradigm is eisegetical at this critical point. While forgiveness may be involved in justification in very restricted situations, it is not inherently part of the justification declaration.

Based upon Abraham's justification model, justification is not a once-for-all transaction.

Since Abraham was justified twice, once for his reception of God's promise of a large progeny and again when he offered up Isaac on an altar, justification cannot be seen as the divine Judge's declaration of a permanent and unchanging status or right standing before Him forever. Rather it is the divine Judge's continuous declaration over a person's actions (responses) every time God observes faith being exercised. Every person will then be justified millions of times during his life if he has walked by faith.

There is only one, spiritual penalty for sin given in the Scriptures although there may be many consequences for any one sin.

The Scriptures are quite clear that the penalty for sin is spiritual death. But there is absolutely no evidence at all that this death includes an eternal condemnation to hell.

Justification is not the same thing nor does it happen at the same time as salvation.

While there is an initial salvation which is different from all the other salvations that will follow it, all justifications are exactly the same. In one sense it is correct to say that *salvation is what God has done through a person, delivering him from sins and temptations, and justification is His affirmation that what was done by man met His standard for righteousness.* But in other senses, justification is God's approval of how the resources obtained from one's initial faith in Jesus are used daily. Furthermore, it is clear that justification took place in the OT, but the gift of eternal life that Jesus offered when He came upon the scene in the first century was never given in the OT. It was a new blessing that God reserves for those who receive Jesus as the Messiah from the time of Jesus to the end of the world.

No one was saved in the OT.

While there is an on-going salvation described in the NT, one from the personal sins and temptations, the main salvation that is described is the future deliverance from the hands of all the wicked, evil people who don't want Jesus (or God) to rule over them. But no one was saved from hell either in the OT or in the NT. Nor is the on-going salvation, present in the NT, ever mentioned in the OT because it involves the life that Jesus gives to those who believe in Him. That life is only offered in the NT.

Salvation has nothing to do with going to heaven.

Not once did Jesus ever relate salvation to the privilege of going to heaven when a person died. While there may be some evidence for an initial salvation, described as the reception of eternal life or of the Holy Spirit, a guarantee of heaven is never attached to either of these gifts. As volume three in this series has shown, no salvation described in the Bible is about going to heaven or escaping hell.

Salvation is only through faith in Jesus Christ.

We have no Scriptural support to believe that the salvation, mentioned in Acts 4:12, can be obtained *through* Jesus Christ *apart from* faith in Him. But it is also a fact that the salvation described there is not about heaven, hell, forgiveness, or justification. It is about physical healing. But all of the other salvations mentioned in the Bible, except one, can be obtained apart from faith in Jesus. That lone salvation is from the time of the coming tribulation upon all the earth.

The saved are not the only ones who go to heaven.

Connecting just a couple of the truths together now, we conclude that heaven is not only for the saved (i.e., for those who have believed in Jesus according to the old paradigm). Many who knew nothing about Jesus in the OT still made it to heaven. As a result, it is impossible to limit heaven to those who have believed in Jesus.

Jesus did not come to start a new religion, but to enhance a former one.

Possibly the greatest travesty of the Reformation and of those who build their theology upon the Reformers is the refashioning of Jesus from a Jewish Messiah into a Savior of the world or into a Lord of all men. In so doing, He has been presented as a founder of a new religion, namely, Christianity. Regardless of how Jesus may have expanded His minis-

140

try, He remained first and foremost the Messiah of Israel. Those who believe in Him have attached themselves to the Jewish faith; they have become proselytes in a sense to Judaism. Jesus came to fulfill the OT Scriptures, both the promises and the covenants that God had given to Israel. He came to encourage people who had believed in the God of Israel. In fact, He taught that *whenever a person believed in Him, that person was really believing in the God of Israel.* So, Jesus did not come to set aside the OT faith; He came to enhance it with new revelation. Setting aside the Mosaic Law is not the same thing as setting aside Judaism since God always intended to set aside the Mosaic Covenant and make a new covenant with Israel in place of the Mosaic Covenant (Jer. 31:27-34). It should be noted however that neither the Mosaic Covenant nor the New Covenant have anything to do with the church age believers in Jesus.

The apostle Paul was never converted.

All my life I have read and heard sermons on the conversion of the apostle Paul. In fact, the first sermon that I ever gave in the ministry was on Saul's conversion to Christianity. That was over forty-nine years ago. I had that perspective because I was taught that whenever a person believed in Jesus, he was converted. And since most of the people believing in Jesus in the Gospels were Jews, I was taught that they had been converted from Judaism to Christianity. That is simply not true. Saul gave his own testimony three times after he encountered Jesus on the road to Damascus and not once did he ever say that he had been converted. *Saul had been corrected and enlightened, but he was never converted.* He was a Jew, and he remained a Jew all of his life. And if Christians don't see themselves as continuing the Jewish faith, they are gravely mistaken.

Saul, who became the apostle Paul, was righteous *before* **he encountered Jesus on the road to Damascus.**

Under the inspiration of the Spirit of God, Saul, now called the apostle Paul, declared in his letter to the Philippian church that he was already righteous *before* he believed in Jesus. This is an insurmountable obstacle to the Reformed, Christian position on justification. Paul didn't need "imputed" (a gifting of) righteousness from Christ as is demanded by Reformed theology. **He was already righteous.** On the road to Damascus, he responded to God's rebuke, believed in Jesus, and was prepared to receive the Holy Spirit through Ananias. But *he wasn't saved (in the sense of Mk. 16:15-16; John 10:9, 27-28; Acts 2:38; 19:1-8) in order to **become** righteous before God. He was already righteous before he believed in Jesus.* And if Saul had rejected Jesus, he would have remained righteous nonetheless. His beliefs and his lifestyle were approved by God as Saul declared to us time and again in his personal testimonies in the Book of Acts and in his letters which are part of the inspired, infallible Word of God.

We have assumed that redemption is from hell.

What we find in both testaments of the Bible is that people are redeemed from life's circumstances; they are not redeemed from hell.

Reading through the Bible from the beginning all the way to the end actually would be enough, I am now convinced, if there was no intimidation, exercised from within our own ranks, to remain faithful to the central theology that we have been taught. The early chapters of Genesis, for example, never once gave the idea that we are taught about man, his depravity, his eternally lost state, etc. Likewise, in the Book of Jeremiah we have most of the doctrines of Calvinism straightforwardly rejected. The only way to overturn the obvious declarations of Jeremiah is to *assume* what is never stated anywhere in the book, namely, that Jeremiah's audience must be part of the so-called category of *unbelievers* (using that term demonstrates a theological commit-ment all by itself). The Bible is sufficient. May we get back to it.

www.ingramcontent.com/pod-product-compliance
Lightning Source LLC
La Vergne TN
LVHW051242080426
835513LV00016B/1713